Remember to talk first with someone and only then about something.

Buntie Wills

This book is a must-have for anyone charged with the responsibility of chairing a meeting, or participating in one in any way. It is written in a clear and accessible style, embedded with gems of wisdom and tips to enhance the vehicles of change and transformation in any organization: meetings. Read it and revitalize your meetings with clarity, and direction.
Dr Nimisha Patel, clinical psychologist and senior lecturer in clinical psychology at University of East London; head of clinical psychology at the Medical Foundation for Victims of Torture; organizational consultant on diversity and discrimination

Meeting Together does what I had thought impossible: it actually makes it fun, absorbing and almost painless to think about and plan a meeting. It is hard not to smile when one reads: "I meet therefore I am" or glances at cartoons poking fun at the ways we tune out during meetings and then engage in righteous diatribes about how that meeting was a waste of time. By getting us to laugh at ourselves and at the meeting game, *Meeting Together* arouses the commitment in all of us to make a difference in the world. As we struggle for social justice and a better world, we spend a lot of time in meetings, much of it unproductive. This timely book enables us to approach each meeting as an opportunity for transformation. It guides us towards building genuine community by the act of simply – and fully – meeting together.
Edgar S. Cahn, PhD, JD, founder and chairman of the board, Time Banks USA; originator of Time Banking and Time Dollars, a local, tax-exempt currency designed to validate and reward the work of rebuilding community

Meeting Together is enjoyable to read, and is an excellent source of advice on helping to keep – or make – meetings or events relevant, valuable, and "fresh". Meetings are so easy to do badly, and the book shows how easily they can be done well. I will use it to help me organize better meetings and events, and also to contribute more effectively as an individual: so it will stay within arm's reach of my desk – for some concentrated reading every now and then, and for inspiration at times of need!
Lyn Adams, PA to the chief executive of Refugee Action and organizer of large staff conferences and other meetings

Over the last 15 years, my colleagues and I have had the privilege of working with Planning Together Associates on many occasions. I have learned each time that a proper process of planning, facilitating and following through makes an enormous difference. George and Lois have unrivalled experience and special skills as practitioners. Their learning is now here for us all to share, in a book to be used and treasured, which can help us all improve the meetings we hold.
Michael Day, chief executive, Historic Royal Palaces

Having run a business and worked with community for almost 30 years I know how crucial a good meeting is to the interconnectedness of the members and the success of an enterprise. Yet most of us learn how to run meetings by painful trial and error. I was thrilled to find in this remarkable book a straightforward and powerful guide to how we can run great meetings consistently, enjoyably and with long-lasting effectiveness. I particularly love the way the book honours not only the job to be done but the people who are doing it. If you spend any time in meetings you'll find this book indispensable.
Dina Glouberman, PhD, co-founder and director of the Skyros holistic holidays in Greece and Thailand and author of the best-selling Life Choices, Life Changes and The Joy of Burnout

At the Centre for Charity Effectiveness we spend a lot of time helping organizations shorten their meetings and make them more effective, so I am sure there is going to be a real demand for this thoughtful but practical book.
Professor Ian Bruce, CBE, Cass Business School, London

We are all familiar with the feeling of meeting overkill. Often, it can seem as if it is just a case of turn up, tune out and drop off. This timely and thought-provoking book equips both facilitators and participants with the skills to get the most out of meetings and reminds us that meetings are about partnerships, relationships, influence and learning.
Rashid Iqbal, asylum advice manager, Refugee Action

A major contribution to a much neglected area of practice – both thoughtful and thorough. A pleasantly high degree of clarity and insight with oodles of guidance for how to make sure meetings are productive. What could be a dry topic is handled in just the right depth to make it eminently usable. A book to be highly recommended to anyone in charge of meetings in the work place.
Dr Janet Summerton, researcher, writer, consultant and chair of All Ways Learning, the continuing professional development organization for people managing the arts

For years I've experienced George and Lois bring complex meetings of disparate people to constructive and inspiring conclusions. All these years I've thought they were working magic. Well if that's so, this book is a step-by-step guide to magic. It is a unique mix of the practical, personal and spiritual. It recognizes that any group of people working together has a life of its own, a life to nourish, train, organize and excite.
Cliff Prior, chief executive, Rethink

Meeting Together is an amazing and excellent book. I particularly like the two active principles, which can be used to transform any meeting: The Meeting Continuum and Two-Way Working. I believe that more time and energy should be given to those principles when the meeting involves people from different cultures and backgrounds. The suggestion in each chapter to "think back" is a very practical idea to help people in their self-learning process.
Van Ly Ung, evaluator, Refugee Communities Oral History Project, Evelyn Oldfield Unit, London

The authors tease, coax and guide readers towards a fresh view of human relationships and social structures, towards a vision that subverts conventional hierarchies of power by making "meetings" not only occasions to imagine and plan transformative action, but occasions to practise a new politics of reciprocity and collaboration. *Meeting Together* turns meetings themselves into revolutionary, liberating, empowering practice – and enables readers to understand why such practice is both necessary and possible, now.
Professor Harold Garrett-Goodyear, chair of the Critical Social Thought Program, Mount Holyoke College, South Hadley, Massachusetts, USA

MEETING TOGETHER

HOW TO TRANSFORM YOUR MEETINGS, CONFERENCES AND OTHER GATHERINGS

Written by Lois Graessle and George Gawlinski

PUBLISHED BY

Lois Graessle and George Gawlinski
Planning Together Associates

Martin Farrell
get2thepoint

PUBLISHED BY

Lois Graessle
1 Magnolia Wharf
Strand on the Green
London W4 3NY
+44 (0)20 8995 0244
lois@planningtogether.com

George Gawlinski
281A Wootton Road
King's Lynn, Norfolk PE30 3AR
+44 (0)1553 671 620
george@planningtogether.com

Martin Farrell
36 Woodbines Avenue
Kingston upon Thames KT1 2AY
+44 (0)20 8404 8661
martin.farrell@get2thepoint.org

www.meetingtogether.org
www.planningtogether.com
www.get2thepoint.org

Drawings by Steven Appleby
www.stevenappleby.com

Design by Marianne Hartley
www.mariannehartley.com

Printed and bound by Biddles of King's Lynn
www.biddles.co.uk

Printed on think⁴ bright paper by Howard Smith.
think⁴ bright is fully recyclable and manufactured from 100% ECF (Elemental Chlorine Free)
woodpulp sourced from carefully managed and renewed commercial forests. The production
mill is registered under the British quality standard of BS EN ISO 9001-2000 and the
environmental standard of ISO 14001.

Graessle, Lois
Meeting Together
1. Management, Planning
1. Title 11. Gawlinski, George
ISBN 0-9528577-2-3

Gawlinski, George
Planning Together
1. Management, Planning
1. Title 11. Graessle, Lois
ISBN 0-9528577-1-5

CONTENTS

DEDICATION

We all first learn about meetings through the experiences we have in our own families. Both of us have drawn on the help of various members of our families throughout the years of creating *Meeting Together* – as readers, editors, sources of stories and of support. We share two pictures of the encouragement we have received from our mothers throughout the writing of this book. On a New Year's Day in a hospital emergency room in Jacksonville, Florida, while waiting for the elder Lois to be admitted to hospital, both mother and daughter could be observed working together on a draft of this book. Whenever we had a writing week in King's Lynn, Norfolk, Natalia would come next door to check on our progress, wondering along with us if we would ever finish the book, and believing in us.

We would like to dedicate this book to our mothers:
Lois Thacker Graessle and Natalia Gawlinski

PREFACE

For the past 25 years we have been in the business of meetings. The great paradox we have observed is that meetings, seen so much as a routine and often burdensome part of our lives, are in fact a vital opportunity for personal and social development and political change. In meetings, together we create both the relationships and the actions whose effects continue far beyond the formal end of the meeting.

As organizational consultants we work with chief executives, boards, staff, international networks and faith and community groups; we have helped them think about their future, plan to turn their intentions into realities, reflect on their progress, design large conferences and talk about personal aspirations. We have done this in organizations ranging from United Nations bodies and major international development and aid agencies with hundreds of staff in dozens of offices to small community groups in which five local volunteers are planning the use of shared play space.

Most of us have some experience of good and even special meetings. We believe that the best meeting you have ever been to could be the kind of meeting that happens most of the time. We have written this book to share the experiences of clients and colleagues and some guidelines, tips and tools to help you find that better place.
Lois Graessle and George Gawlinski

This is not a book about magic. It just seems that way. You see a magician produce a dove from a handkerchief or cut a rope in half and then join it up again. How do they do that?

That is what I wondered when I was a participant in meetings that George and Lois facilitated at the British Red Cross in the early 1990s. Tied up in the tangle of a challenging dynamic, full with currents and undercurrents aplenty, I marvelled at how they brought us through and made it safe and enjoyable – and constructive. How did they do that? It seemed like magic.

Then I started facilitating meetings myself. As I made my first shaky steps I thought about them a lot. I remembered things they had done, simple things like being sure I knew where we intended to be at the end of the meeting before we set out, and like asking everyone to say something at the beginning. And lots more. Simple things. With practice, I became more competent and more confident. I have learnt what can be achieved by people really meeting together.

It is a dream come true for me to play my part in publishing *Meeting Together* with Lois and George and to work with them to help others to transform themselves and their meetings.

The proposition "transform a meeting: change a world" may seem hopelessly optimistic. But it is true that in small, everyday ways we can change our worlds. Magic.
Martin Farrell

TRANSFORM
A MEETING
CHANGE A WORLD

AN INTRODUCTION TO
MEETING TOGETHER

Meetings offer priceless settings in which to learn about ourselves and others as we work together to create and influence our worlds.

Meetings flow out of our experiences from day to day – in our work, in our neighbourhoods and faith groups, even in our families. They are not something we do in addition to being human beings. They are a mirror in which we find out about ourselves as we gather for the business of creating something together.

Yet often we turn meetings into the monsters of our adult nightmares. We devalue them by making them into the object of our frustrations, as something to avoid or cut short, during which to check text messages, make shopping lists, or score points.

Meeting Together sets one of our most common activities, meetings, in the context of one of our deepest yearnings, for a part in a genuine community,

In our work with hundreds of organizations and thousands of individuals over the past 25 years we have rediscovered, with them, ways to have more satisfactory and satisfying meetings more of the time. We have shared those moments of transformation where the huge potential in meeting together is fully experienced.

WHAT DOES MEETING TOGETHER OFFER?
The book invites you to find ways to make your meetings the best of what you have already experienced – more often. It offers you ways to turn meetings from burdens into significant conversations that you look forward to, through:

- A framework for thinking differently about meetings
- Stories, tips, guidelines and examples to help you to create and participate in meetings with more joy and less pain.

WHO IS THIS BOOK FOR?
Meeting Together is a book for anyone involved in any meeting at any time. Whether you are chairing the meeting or attending for the first time, you carry a share of the responsibility for what happens. Each individual has an impact on a meeting, even through the quality of their silence.

WHAT KIND OF MEETINGS ARE WE TALKING ABOUT?

Meeting Together is about meetings of all sorts. Meetings in this book are gatherings in which three or more people are drawn together by a common goal, whether that is to explore an idea or to make final plans for a particular project.

The principles and practical steps in *Meeting Together* are the same for any meeting, whether a routine team meeting or an international conference. In fact, it is routine meetings that are the most important to bring back to life – and the most difficult. If we approach our regular meetings as a burden, we infect and affect our entire organization or network – and our friends and family, too.

WHY DO WE MEET?

We meet when there is something we cannot do by ourselves. We meet when we want help to resolve a dilemma. We meet to be social – and we meet because we are afraid of being left out of the group. Given the pressure of work, we often use meetings just to give ourselves a break. Many of these reasons exist in the same meeting and within the motivation of each participant. That is why we emphasize throughout the book the importance of being clear about the shared purpose that is the theme for any meeting: its momentum will help move disparate people in the same direction.

When a small group of us were planning the first regional conference of small agencies in the emerging democracies in Central Europe, we were trying to express clearly the purpose for such a meeting. One of the group, a pastor and a poet, said that for him the purpose was "to celebrate, to cry, to dream, to plan". We then designed the meeting to bring each of these goals to life.

The possibility for transforming meetings in all these circumstances lies, we have found, in remembering to meet first with people and only then to meet about the business. It is our connections that enable us to sustain the work together. That is why we have titled the book *Meeting Together*, as a reminder that transforming meetings is about working something out – together.

TRANSFORM INTO WHAT?

The mysterious change most of us have experienced in meetings from time to time, from burden to significant conversations, is the alchemy of beginning to transform a random group into a connected community. For ease of use, we have laid out the book as if for a single meeting. Of course one meeting does not build a community. In fact, each meeting is only a part of the process of communicating and meeting and working together over time to create the kind of worlds on which our survival, often quite literally, depends. "Survival" includes survival of our human spirit, as well as survival of our neighbours and our environment.

WHY COMMUNITY?

Human beings live in communities. That's the way we are. In the 21st century the extent to which we achieve things depends on the quality of the communities we create, be they geographic or virtual communities. Communities can differ in their make-up and ways of coming together: creating a meeting space is in itself a dynamic and transformative process. Each time a community is formed we each have to learn quickly and respectfully to create a safe space where communication can flourish. This respect for ourselves and others is a prerequisite for sustained and effective action.

I meet therefore I am

HOW TO TRANSFORM ANY MEETING
THE TWO ACTIVE PRINCIPLES

Two active principles work together to create a meeting in which such transformation is possible: The Meeting Continuum and Two-Way Working.

The Meeting Continuum is the full course of the meeting process, from the first idea to hold a meeting to the final implementation of the outcomes of the meeting. We suggest that 40% of the success of a meeting lies in the preparation, 20% in the meeting itself, and 40% in the follow through.

THE MEETING CONTINUUM 40:20:40
40% Before the meeting we need to:
- **Ask what difference we want the meeting to make**
- **Refine the purpose until we can state it clearly**
- **Create an agenda with precision and space**
- **Make all the arrangements for a nourishing gathering**
- **Finally, but centrally, prepare ourselves to participate well.**

20% During the meeting the challenge is to:
- **Navigate the group's currents and undercurrents**
- **Achieve the purpose of the meeting**
- **Invite that shift that can turn individuals into a community.**

40% After the meeting we need to:
- **Capture and communicate what is different because of the meeting**
- **Act on promises made and decisions taken**
- **Look out for wider, unintended and hidden consequences**
- **Reflect on what we have learnt**
- **Choose to make changes that will make our meetings even better.**

The 40:20:40 guidance is a rough measure of the quality and quantity of attention and mental and emotional energy required at each stage of The Meeting Continuum. Any meeting, however brief or routine, will benefit from this approach.

THINK BACK to meetings you have attended over the past month of so. Has there ever been a moment when, despite an unpromising beginning, something shifted and opened up into genuine sharing? Did you feel connections start sparking or people who had been stuck on different sides of a conflict listen to each other in a different way? Locate just one such experience: the aim of *Meeting Together* is to help you share in creating such an experience more of the time.

If you use The Meeting Continuum to structure your approach to meetings, you will make your meetings more effective and enjoyable. Put the values of Two-Way Working into practice at each stage and you open any meeting to realizing its full potential.

UNCHARTED
TERRITORIES
(NOT TO SCALE)

Two-Way Working expresses the proposition that mutual respect is the heart to unlocking the potential present in any meeting. Two-Way Working implies give and take, a willingness to listen to each other and to find a meeting in the middle.

The phrase "Two-Way Working" came from a story we were told by a friend who was working with aboriginal women in Australia to meet the needs of their community. Initially the white professional women had organized the meetings for the project. When a younger generation of aboriginal women became involved, they began to express dissatisfaction and queried why women from outside their own community organized the meetings. They wanted to organize the meetings themselves and exclude the white women, as they had felt excluded. Instead, one of the elders said to them, "No, we need instead to do two-way working. Find a better way to work together."

Two-Way Working also expresses a paradox: meetings are conversations amongst a number of people. And yet the heart of the matter is one person talking with another – and another and another. Two-Way Working indicates that in order to find a better way to work together, we need to find better ways to have significant conversations with each person we encounter in a meeting.

TWO-WAY WORKING MEANS EXPRESSING IN PRACTICE THE VALUES OF:
Interdependence
We are connected to all other human beings and to our environment.

Individual uniqueness
Each individual is of equal value: we each can enrich a group with our differences and our distinctiveness.

Common cause
Working together, we have the potential to create a practical community each time we meet.

To express these values, we may use our insight and skills to:
• **Include and encourage different voices and perspectives in our meetings**
• **Find ways to include those who are present but silent**
• **Build an environment where conflict between individuals can be acknowledged, contained and sometimes transformed**
• **Design agendas that are purposeful and therefore respectful of people's time and commitment**
• **Listen with our eyes and heart, not just our ears.**

The tips, stories and guidelines throughout the book are practical examples of how Two-Way Working can be expressed throughout The Meeting Continuum.

HOW CAN YOU BEST MAKE USE OF THIS BOOK?

Meeting Together is a handbook to use on your own or as part of your involvement in any kind of group, within an organization, a network, a neighbourhood, or even your family.

At any one time you are likely to be at different stages on The Meeting Continuum with different groups, planning one meeting, attending several more that week, and reviewing the conference you have just been to. Use the book to assess where you are and what you need to do to make each meeting better.

If you want help to have better meetings and at the same time improve your confidence and competence in meetings, on page 84 you will find a practical offer of facilitation, training and coaching. Our website, www.meetingtogether.org, offers more tips, guidelines and other tools, to which you are also welcome to contribute from your own experience.

WHY BOTHER?

Is it hopelessly optimistic to think we can transform a meeting and change a world?

A meeting starts out being a small slice of a world in which power and resources are distributed unequally. These differences within and between people are not going to disappear easily or entirely. Yet we have seen time and again that it is possible to transform meetings into a brief experience of a more hopeful world.

We believe that each meeting is a small sampling of the society of which we are a part, and a small contribution to its health or distress. Are you willing to consider that you have the power to create a glimpse of a better world every time you meet together? Change starts with our willingness to come with even a glimmer of hope that we can make such a difference.

We hope that *Meeting Together* will help you make a world of difference.

THE MEETING CONTINUUM
BEFORE THE MEETING
40%

Before a meeting we ask ourselves what difference we want this meeting to make. Your intentions for a meeting are set in motion when you start to think about it. The quality of the meeting begins as you prepare for it with the mutual respect that embodies Two-Way Working.

We suggest that you invest something like 40% of your attention and energy in this first stage of The Meeting Continuum.

CHAPTER 1
WHY MEET?
Pause before starting to plan a meeting to be sure that a meeting now is really what you need. If so, what kind of meeting do you want and what difference do you want it to make?

CHAPTER 2
DESIGN THE MEETING
Match the purpose of the meeting with the needs and offerings of those who will attend – rigorously and imaginatively, even for a routine meeting.

CHAPTER 3
MAKE IT HAPPEN PRACTICALLY
Make good practical arrangements: they are the critical and equal partner to a good agenda.
Chapters 2 and 3 are a pair: practical ingredients, such as setting a date and booking a venue, go side by side with designing the agenda.

CHAPTER 4
WHY ME? PREPARE YOURSELF
Search through your own skills, habits and expectations to see what you want to take into the meeting. Face honestly what and who make you uncomfortable.

These chapters are intended to help you with the skills of thinking about and preparing for any sort of meeting.

CHAPTER 1
WHY MEET?

FIND THE PURPOSE OF THIS MEETING!

WHY MEET?
AT A GLANCE

To step off the assembly line of deadening meetings, ask yourself:

- Why meet?

- Why meet now?

- How do we decide?

- What kind of meeting do we need?

- Who, when, where, for how long, and how much?

CHAPTER 1
WHY MEET?

Many meetings keep taking place because they always have and no one takes the time to stop and take a look at what is happening. A staggering number take place where the purpose – or purposes – of the meeting are unclear to most if not all of those attending, including the person chairing the meeting.

It is this first question, "Do we really need this meeting?" that opens up the possibilities. Then you can choose whether to have the meeting and, if so, how you might want to go about it. Stop, think, orient and plan: those are the steps. With choice, energy comes flooding back in.

A consultant on organizational development uses this analogy: "You wouldn't ask your staff – or any group of people for that matter – to get on a bus without a destination in mind or without directions. Yet every day people do just that. They gather in a room, close the door and drive around in circles. They call it a meeting."

By the end of this chapter you should have an idea whether you need to get on the bus, what time it is coming, where it is going and who is going to ride with you.

Although the chapter assumes that a lead person (the chair or the senior person) makes the final decision, each person who might be attending needs to check – and voice – for themselves whether the meeting is right for now. Only then will all the information be available. Otherwise, you may find yourself in a meeting with a lot of people, none of whom thinks it is quite right but didn't feel responsible for saying so.

THINK BACK to the meetings you attended during the last month. Were you clear about the reason for each meeting? Did you know what you wanted to be different as a result of meeting together? Were there any meetings that you felt were unnecessary? On reflection, is there an issue for your group that could be dealt with in a different kind of meeting or in some other way?

LISTEN TO
GUT FEELINGS

Go for it!

Uh oh...

One team leader reported that "Our regular team meetings were deadening. We had them every Tuesday, like clockwork, whether we needed them or not. All the business seemed relevant to only half the team: the rest sat in silence. Then one day three of us happened to meet spontaneously at the water fountain and sorted out something in 10 minutes. I realized the difference in energy when you have the right people talking about the right thing at the right time. Now we get clear who needs to meet for what – then every six months we all meet together for a review. We have lunch together once a month – but we don't have meetings we don't need to have."

With practice, going step by step through the following questions need not take long but will save you huge amounts of wasted time and energy.

WHY MEET?

Any group will need meetings for different reasons at different times. There will be legal requirements or funding deadlines or reviews occurring throughout the lifetime of a project.

An experienced chief executive told us about how warily she approaches a request for a meeting. "'Let's have a meeting' always rings a bell with me as it can mean, let's defer a decision or toss it in the long grass!

"I've noticed that there are all sorts of reasons people use meetings to put off doing anything. People are tired and think sitting around a table will give them a bit of time off. There is a difference of opinion and the meeting is for one side to obtain the support of the other, though it is more likely to solidify their separate views. People who weren't at the last meeting don't like the decision that emerged and suggest another meeting to try to obtain the outcome they want. In these and other circumstances, having a meeting could be exactly the wrong thing to do."

What's going on around you will influence when to meet and indeed whether to meet

at all. A coordinator of HIV/AIDS projects in Africa finds that she and her colleagues in non-governmental organizations and in public and government services are facing distinctive challenges in their meetings. "We go to so many meetings that we have no time to follow through on the implications of what we decide. So many middle-level professionals are dying that there are too few of us to carry on the work. Sometimes someone who is crucial to our meeting doesn't show up because they are plugging the gap at another meeting. The solution? We really need to ask ourselves: Do we need this meeting? And who needs to be there?"

WHY MEET NOW?

You may know a meeting will be helpful at some point, but is that point now?

The director of an international education network talked with a range of interested people for months about whether to hold a conference for this new network. "I knew that at some point it would help the network to take off if people got together face to face. But I wasn't sure when – people would need to come from round the world and they would need a lot of notice. And many were teachers so we would have to coordinate about holidays and midterm breaks in different countries. I also wasn't sure yet why we should meet. All I knew was that we would need to meet sometime. I wasn't sure why or who to invite for a long time. So I just kept talking to people and thinking about it until I knew the time was right and then I acted. If we'd gone ahead

What do you need to talk about?
We need to have different conversations at different times.

- Legal requirements and deadlines, for example annual accounts, funding applications, lobbying
- New ideas
- Work in progress
- Challenges
- Shifting social and political circumstances
- Plans for what's next.

What do you need to talk about now?

earlier the timing would have been all wrong. Listening to my intuition worked."

The right meeting at the wrong time is not, in fact, the right meeting. To figure out whether it is the right time requires a combination of information and intuition.

HOW DO WE DECIDE?
First listen to yourself, then talk with others. If you have a feeling that this is not the right time for a meeting: listen to yourself. You are your first source of information, and that information can be your gut feelings. Being worried about something is your insides passing on some useful information.

Voice your feelings, follow them up, don't ignore them. You may find that the reason for the meeting is not yet clear, or the reason that was once so important is no longer valid. Those hunches may also urge you to have a meeting when there is no obvious purpose or they may urge you to postpone a meeting even when the purpose is clear. Just listen.

Talk with others. If you are feeling unclear about the timing or purpose of the meeting, then others are likely to feel the same way. They may also have information that will help you to make the decision. You can save a great deal of time and gain a great deal of

What does the group need?
A group develops through working together.

- At the beginning, to get to know each other and learn how they might work together
- In the middle, to connect in the midst of the pressure of work when people tend to get edgy and lose touch
- Near the end of a project or a year, when people need to stop and appreciate what they've been doing together and say goodbye.

What does the group need right now?

goodwill by checking that the timing of this meeting fits the rhythm for most participants.

Remember to ask people whose role and voice is often overlooked. As one member of an accounts department pointed out, "We are forever being given dates for meetings that fall just on the week we are getting the payroll ready or in the month when we have to complete annual accounts. By the time they tell us, not ask us, everyone else has been invited, arrangements are fixed, and we attend reluctantly and under great stress."

More and more organizations are keeping calendars with major commitments marked for all parts of the organization, in order to put meetings into a logical planning cycle and pace the dates more thoughtfully.

You don't need to make a huge production of this stage: just check out as much as is sensible and manageable and then decide.

WHAT KIND OF MEETING DO WE NEED?
If you think a meeting is the answer, are you clear about what kind of meeting will suit you best?

Meetings that were fresh several years ago can become routine. Organizations need to be flexible and change quickly: consider for each meeting whether there might be a different way to bring the appropriate people together.

A colleague who attends the annual meetings of an international environmental network also cautions against the dangers of getting stale: "When we came up with a new way of running our conferences five years ago, we were thrilled with how much they invigorated the whole network. We had a keynote speaker, themed workshops from each of the sectors (agriculture, gender, drinking water, water for sanitation) and presenters for 15 minutes in each of those. But now the conference has lost its way: every session overruns so people who have come from all over the world to present their case study suddenly aren't given the time.

There is no learning and no dialogue. The purpose has become the conference, not the understanding. We need to meet – but we need to review and renew how we do it. No approach works forever."

It also can take trial and error to get really clear how you need to meet, if you are a group that has many pressures and little time together.

A FACE TO FACE MEETING

A VIDEO MEETING

One manager in a small team described their search to get what they needed: "We all became aware that we were missing the chance just to catch up with each other and this was affecting our ability to manage the agency. So first we tried adding a new item to the agenda of our monthly business meetings: 'Update'. This was first on the agenda and either we went on so long, each reporting on what they had been doing, that other business got squeezed out or, alternatively, we let the check-in slip with the pressure of other business. The solution that finally suited us? Once a week we

stopped at a local café for breakfast together on the way in to the office. This worked even if we only had half an hour; it was better when we could all stay for an hour. We decided our agenda was just three questions: What are you facing this week? What kind of support do you need from the rest of us? Is there anything you are picking up that we need to take seriously for the sake of the agency? Finally we had found a way to keep in touch with each other – and to signal emerging issues so that we could catch them before they became crises."

Do you need a face-to-face meeting or will it work to communicate by phone or video? A meeting has to happen with people at the same time – but they don't have to be in the same place.

Any type of meeting you choose requires particular skills, as the women's officer for the government in Western Australia reminded us: "Out here, phone conferences are a huge necessity because of distances. But you need to chair them skilfully so everyone gets a chance to speak – and so that they don't go on so long that your ear hurts, your arm hurts, and you stop listening. I have one memory where I've gone off, made coffee, returned, and no one noticed."

WHO, WHEN, WHERE, FOR HOW LONG, AND HOW MUCH?
When you are asking yourself and others about a meeting, you will primarily be gathering information about the reason for having this meeting and the specific priorities from different people who might be involved. You will also be picking up information and preferences about when to have the meeting, where, and how long it should be and who might be invited.

You begin to match that information with a budget, in terms of both finance and the cost in time for those arranging and attending the meeting.

At the end of this scan, you will have a sense of the meeting you need and clarity and energy to begin to plan together.

Check minutes of past meetings
Go back to agendas and minutes of other meetings of this group. What items did you carry forward and promise to address "next time"? Does the same item get repeatedly left unresolved? What do you want to do about that?

No business? No meeting!
Set regular dates and only go ahead with the meeting if there are enough items to make it worthwhile – or a pressing deadline.

MEETINGS IN PRACTICE
GUIDELINES

TAKING TIME OUT TOGETHER: AWAY DAYS AND RETREATS

Reflection helps keep individuals and groups healthy. A pause to step out of the rhythm of day-to-day work allows us to check how we are, whether what we intend and what we are doing are still a close enough match, and whether circumstances in the outside world are pushing us to change.

The key to creating successful time out for groups is to find imaginative ways to break out of the daily patterns and organizational habits. Time out offers the opportunity to bring us back into balance with ourselves and our colleagues through:

- **A change of pace**
- **A change of focus**
- **A change of place**
- **A different face.**

A change of pace

Pace the programme so that the rhythm of the afternoon or day or several days feels more expansive than normal meetings. Building in extra-long breaks and walks gives people a chance to meet each other outside the emails and phone calls.

A change of focus

Time out is time for dealing with substantial topics, not for an extended team business meeting. The first task during preparation or even on the day itself is to identify those core issues and find ways of addressing them that are different to the ways you work in a routine meeting. Try banning flipcharts! Look for those topics that are important to the health of your work and working together.

A change of place

Meeting in a different place can change the way we move and think. If you can afford it, time away from the city or town in which you work can offer a huge sense of renewal. If you cannot afford it, there are free places or swaps with another group of their meeting space – or even your own office if you cover up the computers and bring in a special lunch.

A different face

Often an outsider is brought in to facilitate time out. This can free every member of a group to participate equally and discuss more easily issues that are holding them back.

"Why bother? We can't really afford to take the time..." is the response of many people when they are asked to mark a day or more out in their diaries. You can't afford not to. One agency working in the field of criminal justice has a culture of reflection – and at the same time a resistance to taking time out from work with clients. The training officer writes to remind all staff of the purpose of away days: "The agency is a learning organization and is open to new ideas and challenges relating to all aspects of the work... The aim is to clarify our thinking and also to have some fun!" Resistance does not just disappear with a memo: the training officer also helps the planning group to design a programme where the resistance can be reflected on, named and transformed. Often it is about the collective fear of what might change if we were to meet and take time to reflect. Fear, if named and given permission and voice, can also be transformative.

MEETINGS IN PRACTICE
A STORY

A FAITH COMMUNITY TAKES TIME OUT
A member writes of the value of retreat time in their faith community.

Our smallish Quaker meeting, fewer than 30 members, had been using a converted 17th-century pub for meetings. We began to think we might need more space, and commissioned an architect to consider alterations to achieve both a larger meeting room for us and improved facilities to rent to other community groups.

The architect was interested in our ways of making decisions and agreed to work with us on one day of our annual retreat weekend. The four sessions that day each started and finished in Quaker tradition with about 10 minutes of silence.

First, individuals spoke about what it means to meet together as a spiritual community and how the physical fabric of the meeting house contributes to this.

Then the architect asked us to draw places we found particularly inspiring and comfortable. Sketches ranged from a tree house, the beach and a cathedral to the kitchen table. We shared thoughts about the characteristics that made "thin places" – those places at the interface between material and spiritual reality.

In the third session, everyone took chairs onto the lawn to find out how much physical space is needed for 30 people to be comfortable. The architect "drew" around the spaces we created with a rope.

Finally, the architect brought back preliminary ideas about ways the building could be adapted. We were able to agree on a concept that the architect would develop.

The follow through
Some time later the architect came to our regular business meeting and presented us with a plan that we unanimously felt was wonderful – light coming into the meeting room from above, a wild-grass roof, ample storage and space for the children. But the plan cost far more than our original expectations. We had to decide whether to go ahead with the more costly project. First in twos or threes, then all discussing together, we asked ourselves:

Would the development enhance the spiritual life of the community?
Would it improve a community resource?
Did the members have the capacity to raise the money?

In turn, individuals spoke of their hopes and concerns. Each contribution was followed by a short silence. There was no discussion, simply good quality listening. The clerk to the meeting was able to summarize the general view that this was not the right time to proceed, but that we should invest in small improvements, drawing on ideas the architect had suggested.

The solid stable-yard gate is now replaced with coloured steel, offering inviting glimpses of the lighted entrance, and opening up the meeting house to the street.

CHAPTER 2
DESIGN
THE MEETING

DESIGN THE MEETING
AT A GLANCE

To design a meeting requires a balance of art and craft.
The following steps are the same for any meeting; the details
and timings will be different:

- Pin down the purpose and practicalities

- Decide who should be involved

- Think about the group

- Construct the agenda

- Consult, complete and let go.

CHAPTER 2
DESIGN THE MEETING

The most creative part of The Meeting Continuum is arguably this stage of designing the agenda which, for some meetings, is also called the programme.

There are many approaches to designing a meeting: as loose as phoning people to tell them time, place and general idea; as tight as months spent by a planning group for an international conference.

The skills required are like those of a musician. Whether your taste is classical or jazz or folk, you sketch out a theme then return to develop it, adjusting the timing according to the piece, the proposed audience or the acoustics of the hall.

THINK BACK to the meetings in which you have felt most challenged and productive – and the ones that you felt were least effective. What ways of working did you most appreciate, even if you were dubious about them initially? What ways of working made you reluctant to contribute? Decide which ingredients are most appropriate for the meeting you are designing now.

What you can do in a meeting depends on the time available, how well the group works together and the complexity of the work you need to do together. Keep these in mind as you work through the following steps.

PIN DOWN THE PURPOSE AND PRACTICALITIES

When you were deciding whether to have this meeting now, you gathered information. Now as you begin the detailed planning, review what you have learnt and begin the process of turning that information into a meeting.

All aboard!

All aboard WHAT?

A SUMMIT

The step to which we return throughout each stage in preparing for and running a meeting is the clarity of purpose. With a clear purpose, everything else falls into place more easily. You need to express the purpose clearly enough that a 10-year-old can understand it.

One of our most experienced chairs advised: "Get agreement on the purposes of the meeting – sharing information, discussing a policy, thinking about the future. There can be more than one purpose to a meeting. Even so, get clear agreements rather than, 'Let's stick everything in and hope.'"

This is particularly crucial when the meeting is one whose remit is not so clear. Many funders of projects require a group called an advisory group or steering group. Other settings bring together disparate groups into forums and consultations. In such cases, the first agenda that needs designing is the brief for the group itself.

Let's get started...

Inform – NOW
As soon as possible let people know:

- Purpose of the meeting
- Location (the city or area even if the venue is not yet booked)
- Date
- Start and finish times.

The agenda can follow on later.

Consult realistically
Many chairs or organizers approach planning an agenda already frustrated. They have already tried – and failed – to get ideas from their colleagues. As one chief executive said of his small management team, "I email them and ask for any items for our next meeting and they never reply. I am fed up trying to include them." On reflection he accepted it would be better to look for alternative ways of encouraging their contributions. He identified three easy changes he could make in his own attitude and behaviour: to ask people what was on their minds rather then emailing them (they all worked in the same small office and had tea together several times a day), to create a model agenda and use it each time, and to begin the meeting itself by gathering any additional items for the agenda.

Make a shortlist of priorities
You are likely to have a long list of topics that "we must discuss". Turning this into a manageable short list for the agenda is one of the key skills in designing the meeting.

First check whether some items would be better dealt with somewhere other than this meeting, for example in a conversation with another person or by a small group doing research and preparation to present the issue to a later meeting.

We asked a colleague the secret of her informative and manageable agendas. "I have got more realistic about what we can and cannot achieve in our meetings. So I take the long list of priorities and combine items when they have something in common. I also leave twice as much time as I would like when I have picked up that the issue is contentious. I make sure that someone is prepared to introduce the item. I also believe you can get more done if you have proper breaks. I hate going into meetings where you start off feeling that you will never get through the agenda, even if you work through lunch."

Fast forward to the end of the meeting
What do you imagine will be different by the end of the meeting? Fast forward to the end of the meeting and think precisely what this would mean for each item on the agenda.

Consider the difference between:

"Agree our response to the new policy paper on volunteers and name someone to lead on implementing the policy"
and
"Discuss the new policy on volunteers".

Be alert for topics that are expressed in code. "Communication" might mean "How do we keep in touch with each other since we are on the road so much?" or "What information do we need from each other?"

The more precise you can be, the more you will stimulate everyone's energy in the meeting itself.

Give the meeting a name
The name of the meeting matters. Names raise expectations: a "breakfast" meeting implies you will meet early with food; an "away day" indicates you will be away from your office.

Sometimes it helps to choose two names. Combine a description of the kind of meeting with a more inviting, inspirational name, such as:

Human rights have no borders:
The annual conference for all staff.

DECIDE WHO SHOULD BE INVOLVED
The consequences of the meeting in fact start now, not when people show up at the meeting. To identify who needs and who wants to be involved in a meeting and its preparation is a sensitive task.

Who chairs?
Who should chair or facilitate the meeting is not as straightforward as it may seem. Taking the lead has become a confusing role in many settings where democratic ideals may result in power and authority being viewed suspiciously. Often chief executives or senior members of a group feel they should chair because they are "in charge". In fact the role of chairing or facilitating should instead be seen as a role in its own right.

A facilitator or chair is there to look after the process of the meeting, not primarily to contribute to the content. Decide whether an outsider can help you get where you want to, both with the business and with your relationships in working together. If there are powerful and conflicting interests or complex issues, you need the help of a facilitator from outside the organization.

Once you decide who will plan and chair or facilitate the meeting, clarify any other issues about power and responsibility now, or they will surface somehow somewhere anyway, when you least expect them.

Who plans?
From the beginning, at least the person who will be chairing or facilitating the meeting and the organizer need to work together. Their tasks are interdependent in designing the full meeting. Plan together: working cooperatively to plan and organize a meeting can be a crucial factor in its success or failure.

As an administrator in one large organization pointed out: "Involving me from the beginning saves hours and hours of my time. I know what kind of venue is needed; I can alert the chair to considerations about the timing of the meeting because I know better about travel time and dates."

In large meetings and conferences, particularly those involving different teams or organizations, there is enormous benefit in convening a group to plan the event.

Who attends?
If a meeting is to be effective in doing what it aims to do then the right people need to be included. It is so crucial to pause and reflect beyond the obvious.

Sensitivity about invitations to a meeting is about who and how to include people and voices that habitually and silently become excluded in an agency or community's journey. So deciding who should be involved requires preparation

PULLED ALONG BY AN
UNDERCURRENT FROM
ACCOUNTS

by the person chairing or calling the meeting. This preparation includes active and honest reflection on the question of "who is in and who is out... and why?"

Otherwise you may create a meeting that actually perpetuates inequalities and imbalances rather than creating the conditions for change.

Widening the circle of who is included often deepens the challenges in designing a meeting that will be inclusive.

Are you a group that works with users of services? If so, consider how you might include representatives in a way that is genuinely inclusive. A professional member of a government working group described how they learnt to work with members of the group who themselves had learning disabilities: "The group was chaired by a senior civil servant and although the subject was services to those with learning disabilities, the members of the group with learning disabilities very seldom made any contribution. The style and pace of the agenda didn't make sense to them. Finally, we recognized that we were demanding they fit into our way of working, not considering how they might best contribute.

"Instead, before each meeting we asked these two members to interview others in their schools and communities about the topic to be discussed. We then started the meeting with their report back. This had two consequences: they played an active role, and our meeting was transformed by having the information and evidence directly from the clients. By having them start the meeting, we were reminded very forcefully of the whole point of our working group."

Who attends? is a question that needs to be answered skilfully, taking into account where you are going in the meeting and beyond it.

THINK ABOUT THE GROUP
Think about the people who will be attending this meeting. How do you find ways that will take the group beyond the neat, conventional and often deadening forms of meeting? Know yourself, know your group, know the business.

Within the same meeting, individuals and groups can have different priorities about the value of the meeting. A colleague who works with disaster relief in Sudan described the different approaches to their regional meetings of participants from Northern or Southern non-governmental organizations and United Nations agencies: "Those of us from the South are delighted to go to conferences in good hotels where we get a break from the stress of our everyday lives and can network a lot. But our colleagues from the North are more concerned with the programme and getting something formal done – and are much more likely to be stressed about yet another conference." The only solution to such differences is a clear and shared official purpose and pacing to meet the needs of different participants.

As you think about the group, also consider the organizational and environmental culture in which you are working. A client in the Middle East described what they do for meetings: "In Arab cultures, people are used to having a pause in the afternoon because of the heat. So either we start a meeting very early, like 8 a.m., and go on till say 2.30, then have lunch and finish.

Create a planning group
Consider bringing together a group of people to plan any meeting over 12 or so.

Who?
• Chair or facilitator
• Organizer
• Representatives of teams, groups or offices.

What do they do?
• Bring in ideas and information
• Consult their own groups
• Draft the agenda
• Lead sessions
• Train as facilitators.

How?
• Meet once face to face
• Use phone conferences
• Have group meetings throughout the gathering
• Review afterwards.

Such a group gains experience and training in a wide range of skills.

Or we book a hotel and enough bedrooms for the day, start early, have lunch and time out for naps, then reconvene about 5 p.m. when it is cooler."

THE AGENDA

Pick an item out of the hat...

How can you help people to participate?
The aim of the approach in *Meeting Together* is to give the best possible opportunity to involve everyone as active participants rather than disgruntled bystanders. This requires a sensitivity to the difference between stretching people's skills and imagination and pushing them into ways of working that are so uncomfortable as to be counterproductive. The line is a fine one – and finding it often depends on the confidence and skills of the chair and those in the planning group.

When a colleague asked a new group in advance to tell him any ways of working that were particularly uncomfortable for any of them, these were the answers: "group hug", "sports activities", "role play". With that information, he could avoid alienating

members of the group in their first meeting. When people get to know each other better they can become willing to take greater imaginative risks. People often come with resistances based on previous experiences.

None of us knows all the sensitivities of the different sectors and cultures with which we may be working. The best way to ensure maximum involvement of all those attending a meeting is simply to ask what works, and what may not, for them, and listen carefully to their answers. The advantage of planning with a mixed group of people is you can have these conversations during the process of planning the meeting.

What are the currents and undercurrents?
We all know that there are currents and undercurrents among any group of people we work with: the issues that are dominant and those that are consistently ignored as well as the individual and group energies and idiosyncrasies. We feel them and participate in them. We gossip to our friends about them. Maybe we worry and dream about them. Then we ignore them and hope they will go away – or at least stay under the table during the meeting.

Issues that are ignored can be like an elephant in the middle of the room that everyone sees and no one mentions. The "elephant" could be the unspoken knowledge you do not have enough in the budget to do what you are talking about; or that someone is being made redundant and only some people know about it. If you are aware of these undercurrents as you plan the meeting you can make a more conscious choice about how, or whether, to address them.

What methods work best?
As anyone knows who runs meetings or training courses, there are thousands of different methods and techniques for working with a group. We decided not to make a list of these but to include a range in our stories and examples. The main point

is to match the purpose of the agenda item and the nature of the group with a suitable way to work together.

There is a great deal of discussion about differences, whether this means men and women, race or religion, regions and countries. Less attention is given to the fact that we all have favourite and favoured ways of learning and contributing, whatever our gender, national or regional culture. Some people enjoy discussing the principles and philosophy and policies behind an issue; others work better with drawings and diagrams and pictures; others need the precise detail.

A range of styles to suit a range of items will tap into the interest and strengths of different participants, give each person the opportunity to learn – and keep people interested and awake.

CONSTRUCT THE AGENDA

To construct an agenda requires the vision of an architect and the skills of a builder.

In constructing the agenda you are aiming for some sort of alchemy between the business you want to address in this meeting, the people planning and those attending, the hopes and the constraints, the spaciousness and the detail.

A clearly stated purpose, both for the overall meeting and for each item on the agenda, will give direction to a disparate group of people.

A colleague recognized that the skills for designing training sessions and meetings could be very similar. "What surprises me is that in training we know all about telling people what difference this training will make to them and getting people to work in smaller groups and do varied activities – then we come to what we call a meeting and we sit and look at each other and talk for four hours without a break."

Whatever kind of meeting you are planning, you will benefit from taking a rigorous

approach to the design. In Meetings in Practice on pages 24 and 25 we offer a step-by-step approach to designing the agenda in this way.

CONSULT, COMPLETE AND LET GO

Once you have a draft agenda, decide whether you need to consult more widely, get the plan signed off by the senior person, or simply review the draft before sending it out.

If you are consulting, be very clear what you are asking of whom and why. It is better not to consult than to do so and then not have the time or the intention to take those comments into account.

Our main criterion for a completed agenda is that it has the feel of elegant simplicity. Walk yourself through the draft agenda before you complete it for circulation. With experience you will learn to sense when the arrangements and the pacing do not feel in harmony with the business you need to do together. You may recognize, for example, that 15 minutes is not time enough to get people from one building to another for refreshments or that an item is going to take more time than you have allocated. If you fine tune the agenda now, you will avoid many of the delays and difficulties during the meeting itself.

Also remember that whatever and however you plan, this is only one part of the meeting process. A colleague described a meeting of a network of relief agency workers in Uganda: "Although the agenda was planned we arrived to find we needed to change some of the items and the order in which we discussed them. So we sat in the room together and worked our way through what we needed to do together. So I would say, make the plan knowing that you may not want or be able to stick to it rigidly: the plan needs to allow you to be flexible, to balance flexibility and structure."

When you have arrived at an agenda that is ready for circulation, you have completed a critical step in the preparation.

Choose a model agenda
Create a model agenda form. Use it each time for the same meeting – or for all meetings in your organization. You can adapt and change it – or abandon it entirely when appropriate. It will provide you with a familiar starting point every time.

Begin the follow-through now
What happens after the meeting? Decide now:
• Who records
• Who circulates minutes and reminders
• Who needs to be informed.

If you make those arrangements now, you will make the meeting more realistic and the outcomes more sustainable.

MEETINGS IN PRACTICE
GUIDELINES

FIND THE PURPOSE FOR YOUR MEETING: WHAT QUESTIONS ARE WE ASKING?

We meet together to answer questions that we cannot answer on our own. If we all already know the answers, a meeting is probably unnecessary! Knowing what questions to ask, which the purpose of the meeting is to answer, is critical to the successful planning of a meeting. Below we offer a sample of questions that meetings are commonly called to answer. We have structured them around the planning and review cycle that is the subject of our first book, *Planning Together*. Every organization or project or network works to this cycle, however you might express it.

Taking stock
- What's going on?
- What are we learning from our experience?
- What needs urgent attention?
- Are there changes in the political and social context that will affect our work?
- What are our customers or clients telling us? Do we make a difference to them?

Vision
- What kind of work are we intending to do?
- What kind of services do we offer?
- What vision do we have of a better world?

Values, policies and strategies
- Who matters? What matters?
- What principles and values are at the heart of our work?
- How are we reflecting these in our policies and strategies?

Aims and objectives
- What do we intend to achieve? How would we know?
- What direction are we going in this year?
- Are our plans realistic?

Getting organized
- How well are we working together?
- Who is responsible for what?
- What will we do if someone isn't pulling their weight?
- Do we know what risks we are facing?
- Are our financial and administrative systems working well?

Evaluating progress
- Are we making a difference for our clients? How do we know?
- Do we need to adjust our plans in any way?
- What fundamental questions are arising from our work?
- What is the value of our work for funders and how are they measuring us?
- What needs improving?

Why ask questions? Feel the difference between an agenda item that says "Communication" and one that says "How can we use our email, internet, intranet and video links most effectively among our eight offices?" A question opens a door; a statement leaves it closed.

MEETINGS IN PRACTICE
GUIDELINES

CONSTRUCT THE AGENDA

Whatever kind of meeting you are planning, you will benefit from taking a rigorous approach to the design. The steps we recommend are:

1 State the purpose

Express in a sentence or two the purpose of the meeting, in order to include any people new to the group and to ensure everyone arrives with the same expectations. Test whether you could explain the purpose to a 10-year-old. Also state the purpose for each item.

2 Build from a blank timetable

Start realistically. Draw or print a blank timetable. Divide it into squares, e.g. for an hour meeting, 15 minute squares; for a larger meeting or conference, 1.5 hour squares. Remember to put in lines for breaks and meals.

3 Put in key information

First put in any set items. These may include:
- Arrival (check-in, coffee)
- Formal start and ending
- Lunch and breaks.

4 Prioritize skilfully

Look at the list of items you have gathered for inclusion in this meeting. Decide:
- What could be dealt with elsewhere
- What issues need further preparation before putting them on an agenda (assign this)
- What items have immediate deadlines
- What items you need to start considering now in order to make timely progress
- What items can be grouped under the same heading.

Place these items in the squares, giving a notional timing to each one.

5 Bring rhythm to the agenda

Like conducting a piece of music, bring rhythm to the ingredients:
- Put any other business (AOB) at the beginning of the meeting
- Start with an item that seems relatively quick and straightforward
- Put complex or contentious issues early when people's energy tends to be higher
- Make space: ensure there is the capacity to pause
- Avoid stress: set the date for the next meeting before the very end of the meeting
- Allow extra space near the end: if things take a funny turn you will still have time to deal with them before finishing time.

6 Match methods to the topic and the group

Find ways of approaching each topic that match the nature of the topic and what you know of the group, for example:
- Does this issue need discussion in smaller groups? Do we have people confident enough to facilitate such discussions?
- How can we encourage methods of memorable feedback?

7 "Walk through" to the final agenda

Consult where appropriate. Test for clarity, rhythm and spaciousness. Agree the final agenda.

CHAPTER 3
MAKE IT HAPPEN PRACTICALLY

Solid as a rock.

MAKE IT HAPPEN PRACTICALLY
AT A GLANCE

**Attend to the following practical ingredients
in the order that works best for your meeting:**

- **The budget**

- **The date**

- **The place**

- **The food and drink**

- **The people and papers**

- **Potential risks and contingency plans.**

CHAPTER 3
MAKE IT HAPPEN PRACTICALLY

People often talk about the practical arrangements more than they do the substance of a meeting. This is as true for your regular weekly team meeting as for a three-day conference. When people find no papers, refreshments not on time, the rooms dirty or locked, the difference is only one of scale; the effect on the atmosphere for the meeting is similar. People don't feel valued; already the meeting is devalued.

A bit of pampering goes a long way to create an environment that will nourish a productive meeting. Pampering can mean how people are greeted on arrival, whether the chairs are comfortable, or simply whether there are alternatives to tea and coffee, or that someone has put the biscuits on a dish rather than leaving the torn-open packet on the table. All of these touches convey a message: "You matter and we welcome you."

THINK BACK to the last meeting you attended. When you walked into the meeting room, what message did you get? What do you remember about the practical arrangements – in advance and during the meeting? What do you remember about what you discussed? What effect did all these arrangements have on your participation? Now create a picture of the environment you want for your next meeting.

To make the meeting happen fully, even a small and routine meeting needs someone responsible for the arrangements. The organizer needs the time to do what is needed, time officially recognized and negotiated as part of their job, and the resources to do the job well. How much money is there to spend? Who can they call on for help? Who is in charge? Who is planning the agenda?

Consider the preparation for any meeting as a partnership between the planner, whether chair or chair and planning group, and the organizer. Together they need to draw up a timetable for all the work that needs to be done for a meeting. This is especially true when an external facilitator or event organizer is involved. An example of the

interdependence of programme and arrangements is the story from one client who attended a conference sponsored by an international agency. "I discovered that they had spent hundreds of thousands of dollars yet few of the delegates were from the regions whose problems we were discussing. They had not been invited in time to get visas to travel to the conference."

The order in which you attend to the practicialities will depend on the culture and circumstances of your group: you may do some before designing the agenda or alongside that process. Decide that as part of your overall and initial planning.

THE BUDGET

Meetings cost. They cost in venue and transport and in the time for preparation and attendance. However your group gets the funding for a meeting, take the time to work out what it will really cost. In some commercial organizations, a special clock is activated when the meeting starts. It calculates the cost of each person's time and how much the meeting costs. It is worth bearing in mind that our time is of value. A colleague new to staff conferences admitted that he was vociferous in attacking the cost. "I could only see that we could have 10 new computers for what these two days would cost. But when I attended the first one and saw what difference it made to meet with colleagues whom I otherwise only talked to about their IT problems, I was convinced."

THE DATE

Think about the date in good time: one great source of wasted time is meetings that happen too late – too late to respond to a new policy initiative, too late to give feedback on a plan threatening major community upheaval, too late to catch financial problems before they escalate or a funding application before the deadline.

There will be complications about dates whatever the group. The convenor of a village hall committee in a rural community said that when she was checking a series of dates for meetings to work on their funding application to renovate the village hall, "I discovered that the first date clashed not only with half-term but with a critical time in haymaking for those who were farming families and another date with a big conference for one of our group who works part-time at the university. It was interesting how I got the information – those from farming families didn't have diaries but knew their seasonal commitments; others had to look in their diaries."

Dates not made in time can often exclude people you want to attend.

THE PLACE

Once you have a sense of the purpose of the meeting and how many people are likely to attend, you can look quite imaginatively at where you might meet. Unless you are clear about the purposes, you may waste a lot of time discussing venues for a two-day retreat when all you need for this meeting is a comfortable room for a couple of hours of planning.

The venue itself can enliven or depress. As one trainer said of her search for a venue for away days for a very stressed team, "I was looking for a place that had the feel of cherishing them after the bad experience we'd last had in a dreary room. We had left it too late to find anything better." She found it: an old house, a garden and the quality of food helped the participants to relax and deal with some difficult issues.

Where could we meet?

Make a list of what you need from the venue, then consider places that meet these criteria. It is here that cooperation between the agenda designers and the organizer are critical. A meeting that needs people to sit around tables in a big room in order to discuss some difficult issues will be jeopardized if the organizer has gone ahead and booked the usual theatre-style room with fixed seats. As a colleague says, "You can always tame a venue, but it is certainly better to get it right in the first place."

How do you calculate the cost of a meeting? Estimate the real cost of a meeting. Check:

- What is the average hourly salary or wages (or estimates, for volunteers) of those attending? (Multiply by the number of people attending.)
- How many hours is it likely to last?
- What is the cost of:
  - Venue
  - Refreshments
  - Travel
  - Replacement staff?

Bear in mind the intangible benefits you would gain from meeting.

THE FOOD AND DRINK
Even the briefest of meetings benefits from refreshments. What is appropriate? What can you afford? Some people never drink coffee; some only drink coffee. Some need a mid-morning snack; others are diabetic and cannot have sugar. And all will remember the refreshments even if they may forget some of the discussions. At the very least, people need water to feed the brain.

THE PEOPLE AND PAPERS
Once the agenda is completed, there are a number of final steps in the arrangements.

Invite enticingly
More and more organizers of meetings are finding that some people don't respond to emails or even phone calls about meetings. Organizers are looking at ways of contacting people about meetings in more creative and effective ways. One consultant who is also an artist enthusiastically makes invitations to meetings as a work of art: "We have sent postcards of the seaside, inviting people to the conference centre on the coast; we have made cards and menus and put secret messages in people's pigeonholes. I feel really strongly that if we want people to come with some enthusiasm and anticipation, we need to entice them. And I have found that if they see you have put yourself out, they are more willing to make some effort as well."

Brief presenters, contributors and facilitators
Some of the best-planned meetings falter in practice because people have not been briefed effectively about their role. As the planning group for one large conference recognized, "Some of our workshop leaders talked for 90 minutes: for the next conference, we asked them to leave time for people to participate, at least by asking questions, and we gave them a facilitator from our planning group, to agree with them how to keep time."

We too often treat honoured guests as hands-off contributors. Instead, it can be more respectful of them and of the meeting to brief them about what you want; negotiate clearly about how much time they have and let them know you really need them to stick to time in order to achieve the overall purpose of the meeting.

Find the place, see the space
Make a list of what you need from a venue. Then look imaginatively for a place that suits your needs and your budget.

While you are planning walk through the venue with your meeting in mind. If you cannot visit the venue in advance, see if they have a tour on the website. Or arrive early on the day to avoid surprises and hiccups.

Gather requests and needs
Make your own list of the particular needs people invited to this meeting might have, including:
- What they can and cannot eat and drink
- A special room for prayers
- What support people with hearing or sight impairments might need
- Who needs help with the language, with translation or interpreters.

The preparation of information for a meeting – the agenda, any necessary background papers and information – is a signal of the seriousness with which people's contributions are being requested.

Keep people informed
Consider some of the reasons advance notice can be helpful and where lack of

it can be excluding and disrespectful to those invited to participate.

Participants may need to consult with the colleagues they represent; people whose first language is not the language of the meeting may need more time to read the papers and agenda; people with a range of physical challenges will have the time to prepare; some clients and users of services may need time to prepare.

Lack of information can affect the trust in the group. One friend who serves on the board of a faith centre tells about the discrepancy between their intention to be collegiate and the experience of budgeting meetings. "Most of us felt very manipulated yet again in the budgeting process. The relevant papers were handed out the same night we had to vote on them. The chair knew no one wanted a five-hour meeting for going through the budget; he banked on us giving the budget a quick pass instead. I don't think he and the finance team were being fiscally irresponsible, just that they dreaded the hassle of all of us amateurs questioning them. But the process produced a lot of ill will about how we were unable to carry out our fiduciary responsibility because we had not been given papers in ample time."

Prepare papers in time
The organization of papers for meetings is an art form. What papers do people need in advance – and what are they expected to do with each one? Tell them: this can make a huge difference to their participation.

Look at the quantity of papers and predigest them, not only to make preparation manageable but out of respect for trees. It takes time to shorten or summarize a paper, but doing so will save time and gain goodwill for the meeting.

As one colleague from Vietnam said of the thick pile of papers he got for a board meeting, "With my English not so good, the only way I could take in these papers was to burn them, mix the ashes in water and drink them!"

POTENTIAL RISKS AND CONTINGENCY PLANS
The purpose of meticulous preparation is that having done what you can you are free to attend to the unexpected.

There are limitless possibilities for external circumstances to affect your careful plans: some are life and death risks, others are inconveniences.

Colleagues from London en route to a long-planned conference in Colombia got the message in Miami airport that they were to turn back: an aid worker in another agency had just been killed and the sponsors did not want to take a risk. Bomb scares regularly delay transport in many cities.

For a big event or one in which people are travelling or costs are high, it may help you to make a list of the possible risks, ways in which you might prevent at least some of them happening, and remedial action to take if they do happen.

Why bother?
Why bother with all this preparation, especially for small and routine meetings? Why not just leave things till the meeting itself? Preparation gives us the possibility of a better meeting and reflects the value we place on others.

Support plain speaking
Use plain language for the agenda and any papers. Avoid initials, shorthand, first names, jargon. They create insiders and outsiders before you even get to the meeting.

Spell out the full name the first time you use it, e.g. United Nations (UN).

MEETINGS IN PRACTICE
A STORY

A GATHERING OF AN INTERNATIONAL NETWORK

Two hundred people representing more than 100 independent organizations from 20 countries are members of a pan-European human rights network serviced by a small secretariat. At a turning point in their own history and in that of European politics, they came together for four days. Their aim was to agree positions on key policies that would steer the work of the secretariat over the next three years.

The consultative process was rigorous and led to some clear policy directions and a fantastic sense of community. What were the ingredients?

BEFORE THE MEETING
Clarity of purpose

The secretariat and its board worked together to discern the essential purpose of the gathering. Was it for policy development or policy confirmation? They felt that wide involvement by participants from all parts of the expanding network would enhance the quality of relationships as well as the quality of the policy directives themselves. Working from this principle, it became clear that policy options drafted in advance should be used as aids to significant discussions among everyone rather than decisions to be ratified.

Planning and preparation: Programme and arrangements

Paradoxically, in order to create an environment that feels open and responsive, meticulous planning is necessary. Preparation included assigning everyone to groups in advance, checking accommodation, checking the need for interpreters and translators and sending out papers. A great deal of work went into getting the consultative policy papers brief and clear.

Creating a core community of facilitators and recorders

One secret ingredient for success was the team of volunteer facilitators and reporters (called "rapporteurs") who reviewed the draft programme during their training. Funding was provided to bring the facilitators from their different countries together for a day's training. They also met as a group with the conference consultants regularly throughout the conference, to ensure the conference stayed finely tuned to the needs of participants and was alert to issues emerging. As one facilitator said, "I had no idea what I was volunteering for – which was probably a good thing! It was non-stop hard work – but we supported each other, achieved what we set out to do, and I learned more than I remotely imagined about working with groups."

DURING THE MEETING
A surprise beginning

Participants arrived expecting to start with formal opening ceremonies in a conference hall. Instead they were met by facilitators and organized into their small mixed "home base" groups over coffee – introducing themselves, their organizations, their concerns – before joining others for a formal plenary. As one of the original founders of the network said about this informal start, "This was the first time I have been to a conference and spoken to anyone outside my own clique – and that was because we started by getting to know strangers."

Using assorted groups and methods

Home base groups met at the beginning and end of each day. Each chose representatives to the various policy groups based on interest and experience. The policy development groups drafted policy positions, which were then discussed in home base groups throughout the conference. Ad hoc groups posted their interests on the notice board and arranged meetings as additional working groups.

For the final gathering, policy development groups were requested to design presentations that were brief and made the key points in a visual, unusual style. They also drafted papers for the secretariat to use as a basis for final policy work.

Facing the (almost inevitable) crisis

Facilitators and the policy group rapporteurs spent most of the hours of the night preparing the draft policy papers and designing flip charts and other displays for the group presentations on the last morning. Just as everyone was assembling for a 9 a.m. start, the facilitators discovered that the flip charts were missing. After a massive search, they were recovered from rubbish bins. By 9.10 the flip charts were back, everyone was seated and the prime minister of the host country walked in to address the final session.

Ending creatively and passionately

How could 200 participants each comment on every policy recommendation without turning the plenary into a nightmare? A system was devised whereby, after each policy presentation, questions were only taken for clarification. All participants were then given five minutes to fill out a comment sheet: what I support in the policy proposal, what I feel unclear about – and what I oppose.

After the conference the secretariat used these comment sheets to develop further drafts of the policies. This system gave people the confidence that they had a genuine say in all the emerging policies, not just the one their own group had considered.

During the final session the secretary-general praised the volunteers who had worked so hard to pull the event off. The comments might have seemed like one of those remarks in passing but in practice volunteers felt it a great honour to be mentioned so publicly.

The secretary-general ended his final keynote speech by capturing the atmosphere of passionate involvement during the gathering. He pledged that the secretariat would play its full role in the coming years in realizing the aims and ambitions of the total organization as manifested in the conference.

AFTER THE EVENT

On reflection

People came away from the meeting with a positive attitude, even the original members who had for many years run these big meetings in a different way. The position papers that were produced by the secretariat, based on conference discussions, had greater agreement and led to deeper and broader discussion and lobbying in each country. The secretariat experienced the effects of a greater commitment and involvement among members in other forums in the years that followed. There was a greater willingness to try out new ways of working together.

As one member of the secretariat summed it up: "Plan well. Work hard. Reap rewards."

CHAPTER 4
WHY ME?
PREPARE YOURSELF

WHY ME? PREPARE YOURSELF
AT A GLANCE

Before any meeting, pause however briefly to ask yourself:

- **Why am I going to this meeting?**

- **What difference can I make?**

- **How can I prepare for the business?**

- **How can I prepare myself to work with this group?**

- **Can I prepare for the unexpected?**

CHAPTER 4
WHY ME?
PREPARE YOURSELF

Meetings with yourself – and meeting yourself – are at the heart of *Meeting Together*. Any group is a collection of individuals trying to do something together. The needs, skills – and attention – of each individual determine the quality and the sustainability of any gathering.

As we have come to treat meetings as objects marked in diaries rather than opportunities, we have come to forget the impact we make on any meeting we attend – and it on us. In this chapter we reflect on ways in which you might reconnect with what the point is for you.

THINK BACK to a recent meeting that still preoccupies you in some way. What aspects of your contribution did you feel good about? When did you feel uncomfortable? What do these different experiences tell you about yourself and what you might need to attend to before the next meeting?

There are a number of questions you might want to ask yourself as you prepare for the meeting you are about attend.

WHY AM I GOING TO THIS MEETING?
We usually have two sorts of reasons for going to a meeting: the formal and the informal. Both are legitimate. It is likely to help both your preparation and your participation if you can be clear with yourself about both.

What is the formal purpose of this meeting for you? What is your informal agenda?

A routine meeting needs as much attention as a big gathering, perhaps more. It is in such meetings that you will be meeting time and again with the same colleagues: this gives you a great opportunity to see relationships that might want attention and habits that may need challenging. Start with your own habits as those are the only ones we can be sure we can do something about.

Reflecting on her dissatisfaction with weekly department meetings, a client finally realized what she had been doing in the weekly meetings since a merger of departments with which she had disagreed. "I would arrive late to meetings, sometimes not even show up and not ring, and certainly not prepare by reading the agenda. When I was thinking about how angry I still was with the chair who led the merger, I saw that my own behaviour simply diminished me and sabotaged the work. And that there might be a more adult way of addressing my continuing concerns. So I started by showing up on time!"

Life is rarely as you want or plan for it to be. You may have no choice but to attend a meeting, however unclear and inappropriate you may think it is. Look for even the smallest way to make it worth your while, even if not as part of the formal meeting.

One of a group of community workers in Wales describes how they struggled to come to terms with a regular meeting

that they felt they had to attend to keep their funding secure. "We met together and agreed some issues we wanted on the agenda. Because we had established a good relationship with the person drawing up the agenda, we had more hope that some of these issues would actually be discussed. It didn't work perfectly – but it did break our cycle of moaning about the meetings."

The attitude with which you enter the door for the meeting has a subtle – and sometimes not so subtle – impact on the atmosphere you share in creating. You have choices, always.

WHAT DIFFERENCE CAN I MAKE?

There are a variety of ways in which you contribute to a meeting. Depending on the size of the meeting, you may find yourself playing more than one role: chair and organizer, presenter and participant, participant and minute taker.

You may find the lists on page 40 a helpful place to start in reviewing what roles you might be playing in a meeting.

We are in the habit of thinking that most if not all the power and responsibility in a meeting lies with the chair. The influence of the chair or facilitator in both obvious and subtle ways is undeniable. Can you make a difference as a participant?

A central message of *Meeting Together* is that everyone influences a meeting. The possibility of turning a disparate group of people into a community lies with each person taking their share of responsibility.

It is particularly important for participants to recognize the parallel set of roles we play in helping the group work together towards its agreed goal. The informal roles we play in a meeting and the way in which we behave are often more powerful in their effect on the meeting than the formal roles. Do you find yourself encouraging the quieter ones to speak? Are you good at picking out the key points when the discussion seems to

be going around in circles and even the chair is obviously lost?

Whatever your roles, you have work to do to prepare yourself. At one of our courses on meetings, a participant asked how she could make her voice heard when she was usually the youngest, the most junior in status, and among a minority of women. By the end, she had decided, "I need to have confidence that I have a contribution to make and be prepared for that. One way I can make my presence felt is simply to ask questions of the others, to clarify, to help us all stay on track, to bring in elements through questioning that they might not have considered. To do this, I need to remember to breathe!"

A wise and skilled chair will encourage a group that meets regularly to have some sort of induction for new members, in order to introduce them to the way in which the group works and the ways in which they can best contribute. One planning group for their annual staff conference for 200 people realized that newcomers often felt lost, both practically and emotionally. In fact, many reported they got headaches the first time they attended the big gathering. "We have

Telephone if you are anxious
If there will be someone you don't know at the meeting, or perhaps someone you feel uneasy about encountering for some reason, phone them in advance, just to make the connection.

What shall I wear?
Be comfortable with yourself so that you will contribute more comfortably. What you wear gives signals – of your respect for the customs of a group or country, of your care for yourself. Just be aware and choose.

had several ways of trying to make people more welcome. First we asked their teams in advance to tell them a bit about what the conference was like and to pair them up with someone in their team to ask questions. Then on the first night after dinner, we had a special session just for newcomers and the members of the planning group. A few games so people would know each other, a walk through the map of the conference centre. People enjoyed the attention, they said."

HOW CAN I PREPARE FOR THE BUSINESS?

To prepare for the business of the meeting you need to know what it is about and what you hope to achieve. You may have been sent an agenda; you may not. If you still are not clear when you reach the meeting, ask the chair. It's your time you are spending so don't waste it.

Let's work together.

In preparing for business you may need to:
- Read and make notes on the agenda if one is sent in advance
- Gather information: What you need from others and what you need to bring
- Prepare to introduce an agenda item or present some information

- Make your arrangements realistically: How to get there and by when
- Prepare for your role by consulting team members or contacting members of your group if you are facilitating.

Sometimes we may need to prepare on our own and at other times we may need to work with others in advance of the meeting to give ourselves the best chance of being individually and collectively effective.

Some people are quicker in meetings than others – and can rely on this rather than on preparation. A friend admits that she seldom took time to read papers in advance. "Instead, I know I rely on my quickness in groups and, quite frankly, my charm. But after hearing the concept of 40:20:40, I thought I'd try reading all the papers for my next meeting. I was amazed at the difference in my confidence and contribution. Not so much of talking off the top of my head and I was more able to listen genuinely to the others. It was as if I had studied the map in advance rather than just getting in a car and setting off."

HOW CAN I PREPARE MYSELF TO WORK WITH THIS GROUP?

Each of us comes to every meeting with history and attitude. We have had experiences in other groups and in our families that affect how we behave in groups.

Look at yourself in your group mirror. What do you know about yourself and your style of participating? An organization is in fact a bit like an extended family: we all bring into our work, however consciously or unconsciously, values and approaches that we learnt in our birth families and neighbourhoods.

You might want to reflect on the last meeting of this particular group. How did you feel when you left the meeting? What did you observe about yourself? What skills did you use effectively? Where did you feel you hadn't behaved as you had intended? Has anything happened since the meeting to affect your participation in this one?

OUT OF YOUR DEPTH

Face in yourself what you might be afraid of – conflict, for example, or what your boss may think of you. Or pay attention to the person you feel uncomfortable with, or the issue that you know you get emotional about. Just walk yourself through both the agenda and the group; see if you can feel and sense the areas and issues that might trigger your own vulnerabilities – and strengths.

"Our best hope of transforming a meeting is to connect with and work with the people we are most afraid of", one reader emailed, adding that she had finally phoned someone she was dreading meeting again, just to make that personal contact and quit seeing her as a threat.

If you do discover that you are feeling in conflict with someone who will be attending the meeting, you may want to address that

before the meeting. The words we speak are only 10-15% of what we communicate. If something is bothering you before a meeting, the difficulty will be there at the meeting too, whether you say anything or not.

The guidelines on page 40 offer a checklist of possible roles and behaviours.

CAN I PREPARE FOR THE UNEXPECTED?

Something unexpected is almost guaranteed to happen on the day of the meeting itself. The unexpected might be an external event, such as arrangements that change or fail or an emergency item for the agenda. The unexpected might also be a surprising or shocking development between people in the meeting, unexpected decisions or an outburst from yourself or someone else that seems to come from nowhere.

A mood can emerge quite unexpectedly in a meeting, unexpected to both the speaker and to others. We cannot prevent such mood shifts in a meeting; we can prepare ourselves by knowing better our own mood shifts and therefore being more able to participate effectively during the meeting.

An experienced facilitator for a day-long meeting described the mood shift that occurred after lunch. "As chair I made a classic mistake after lunch and went on and on – and on. I felt people getting angry; I saw others nodding off. Finally, I recognized what was happening, stopped, told them all to take a break while I reflected on what to do. When they came back we had a quick discussion on what had happened – then got on with the business in a more lively way. In the feedback at the end, several participants said the mood was transformed by my admitting my mistake, pausing and doing something about it."

It is in interaction with both ourselves and with others that we find out who we are. A meeting offers a wonderful opportunity to develop our own awareness and, in doing so, to contribute to a more satisfying meeting.

Immediately before the meeting
Pause for at least five minutes to make the transition into the meeting:

- Make any necessary calls then turn off your phone
- Gather your papers: glance at them quickly
- Take a deep breath
- Remember why you are there
- Leave enough time to meet people informally.

Now you will have arrived more fully.

MEETINGS IN PRACTICE
GUIDELINES

We have a choice about how we contribute to meetings, in formal and informal roles and in our behaviours. Here are three lists that might help you get clearer about what you might be doing in the meeting.

FORMAL ROLES YOU MIGHT PLAY
Consider what formal roles you usually play in a meeting. How competent do you feel?
- Chair
- Organizer
- An outside consultant, facilitator or trainer
- Participant
  - Representing your team or organization
  - Attending in your own right
- Other roles in planning and attending the meeting
  - Facilitator for a group discussion or workshop session
  - Recorder or minute taker
  - Member of a planning group
  - Presenter for an individual item on the agenda or programme
- Roles for those who are not attending
  - Briefing your representative
  - Taking care of practicalities.

INFORMAL ROLES YOU MIGHT PLAY
Observe yourself at the next meeting. Which of these informal roles do you find yourself playing?
- Encouraging others to speak
- Clarifying points in discussion
- Summarizing
- Raising points of discomfort and undercurrents
- Signalling when it is time for a pause.

BEHAVIOURS YOU MIGHT RECOGNIZE
You might want to scan this list and see if you recognize any of your own behaviours in meetings: add others you will admit to. Most behaviours represent something we are not saying. Is there a more constructive way you can make the point?
- Always come late. Either don't apologize at all, just create a disturbance looking for a seat, or apologize profusely
- Talk across the group to one particular person, raise your eyebrows or wink knowingly
- Do urgent work – flip through diary, edit a paper, write a letter – during the meeting
- Keep looking at your watch and yawning
- Never volunteer – just criticize those who do
- Use 25 words if two will do
- Always leave early
- When bored, tell a funny story, pass the biscuits, ask when coffee is coming
- After moving to the next topic, bring up a point about the previous topic
- Write notes to person next to you – or pass to a person on other side of room
- Never say anything (until the meeting ends and then you moan to friends)
- As chair, when someone else is speaking, do crossword puzzles.

MEETINGS IN PRACTICE
A STORY

MEETING THE UNEXPECTED: A PIVOTAL 47 MINUTES
The organizer for a complex international gathering describes an unexpected meeting.

I expected an informal meeting with two or three people in the City Hall Security Department in Belfast to talk through the arrangements for a visit of the Dalai Lama and the president of Ireland to the building, an occasion bearing powerful symbolic meanings. I walked in and, to my horror, almost 30 people were sitting silently around a large conference table – representatives of the Royal Ulster Constabulary and the different political groups, the City Hall chief executive with staff and community representatives. And I was on my own, without an agenda.

"Help!" I said to myself, as I sat down at the head of the table.

My aim for this meeting was to identify problems that might arise from the visit, and then to win the support of the necessary people in finding practical solutions. But this now had to be done in the setting of a formal, but completely unprepared, meeting.

Although I had faced opposition to our plans, I entered the room completely hopeful, believing the integrity of what we were trying to do would somehow see us through any problems that arose.

After the initial feeling of utter panic, I was aware that I had been through terrible meetings in the past and that I must have a reservoir of experience to draw on. The absence of an agenda actually helped: people had to listen to me, which helped me get across the broad sense of the task, rather than focusing on details on a written agenda.

I think people responded to my being honest and open and this was better than trying so hard to persuade them. I was conscious of drawing on some basic skills, like making sure that everyone had a chance to have their say and reflecting back to the group what had been said. At the end of each point I would say, "We appear to have agreed on this. Does everyone agree?" But it was about facilitating rather than control. I simply tried to help everyone listen to each other carefully and let our common interest emerge. There were all kinds of specific interests present in the room; but somehow we discovered an area of common interest.

Just 47 minutes after I'd walked into the room, I found myself with a group transformed in the most unlikely circumstances. I was astonished and relieved to find we had got full agreement from everyone there.

Meeting the unexpected is about preparation and the importance of being prepared. At first glance this story might seem to be saying you can turn up unprepared and, by busking it, succeed beyond your wildest dreams. In fact the ways in which the organizer was prepared emerge clearly in the story – he knew what mattered and what must be achieved, he knew what his strengths were, and which skills to use. And he succeeded by ensuring that people had an authentic encounter with him and with each other.

THE MEETING CONTINUUM
DURING THE MEETING
20%

A meeting is an invitation into the unknown, however clear-cut the agenda.
If you approach with curiosity, you will be better able to contribute to deeper,
wider and more unexpected solutions and resolutions.

This is as much a challenge for a routine meeting as for a special event.

CHAPTER 5
NAVIGATE THE CURRENTS AND UNDERCURRENTS
provides a structure for moving together through any agenda, mindful of both the
official purpose that has brought people together and the currents and undercurrents
that will affect its outcome.

CHAPTER 6
INVITE GENUINE COMMUNITY
explores key elements that help a group of people to transform the experience
of working together into more than the sum of its parts.

These chapters describe Two-Way Working in practice in meetings.

CHAPTER 5
NAVIGATE THE CURRENTS AND UNDERCURRENTS

NAVIGATE THE CURRENTS
AND UNDERCURRENTS
AT A GLANCE

There are three key parts to any meeting, no matter what its length, purpose or style:

GET STARTED
- **Arrive in time**
- **Welcome informally**
- **Introduce everyone formally**
- **Remind and renegotiate**
- **Make judgements about time and timing**

WORK THROUGH THE AGENDA TOGETHER
- **Create genuine safety**
- **Navigate the content**
- **Balance task and group**
- **Hold the tensions**
- **Decide on action: record decisions**

FINISH WELL
- **Plan for action and follow through**
- **Leave time for loose ends**
- **Reflect, appreciate and say goodbye**
- **Be alert to postscripts.**

CHAPTER 5
NAVIGATE THE CURRENTS AND UNDERCURRENTS

A good quality meeting results from steering the group effectively through ordered conversations (currents) whilst being responsive to the needs and idiosyncrasies of individuals and the rhythms of the group (undercurrents).

Imagine a ship's journey. The destination is clear, the course is set – and only by responding to the winds and the waves does the captain have the possibility of getting the ship there safely.

Or picture a family or friends cooking a meal together. They know the menu but everyone throwing in their own pinch of this, spoonful of that will create that distinctive meal.

Even though you have used the same recipe many times, you still cannot count on that cake or casserole tasting the same each time. A meeting is like that: our experience is likely to have taught us that our biggest contribution may be to show up and pay attention.

THINK BACK to the last meeting you attended. Did you feel there were points at which people were genuinely talking together? How well balanced were the tasks on the agenda and the rhythm and energy in the group that day? What role did you play in moving things along? What role did the chair play? For this meeting, decide what you want to do differently yourself.

There are four partners in a meeting – the person chairing and the others attending, plus the agenda and the venue. An effective meeting is like a dance amongst all four, one partner taking the lead at one point, another as the rhythms change.

GET STARTED
The first task is to get everyone there – in body and spirit and remembering what the meeting is about.

Arrive in time
For the chair and the organizer, the meeting begins well in advance of the arrival of participants. Once you check that all the equipment, materials and refreshments are available and the room is properly arranged, you will be free to greet participants. And you will have dealt with last-minute surprises.

Early arrival pays off in unexpected ways. One of our colleagues arrived for a four-day event to discover that the room they had booked, the only room available, was still being painted. The centre planned to have it finished by the time the meeting started – and couldn't understand her concern about the effect of toxic paint fumes over an eight-hour day. Because she was there early they could work out alternatives (the ballroom until it was needed for a wedding, then the breakfast area). This turned a potential disaster into a logistical challenge.

Welcome informally
The meeting begins when people walk in the door. The welcome, the refreshments and the arrangements give signals about the hospitality behind the agenda, and can prevent problems during the meeting.

One department at a college of further education used this informal time to break a habit in their meetings, in which the style of doing business was antagonistic and often verbally abusive. Several members who were concerned about this destructive pattern decided to offer their room for coffee and sandwiches half an hour before the meeting. "The very fact of people meeting up informally with each other as people – before we stepped into the roles that had become like set pieces in a battle plan – changed the quality of our formal meeting enormously."

Pay particular attention to people who are attending for the first time.

Introduce everyone formally
There are dozens of ways to start a meeting: the approach you choose needs to make sense to the purpose of your meeting and the nature of the group, or people will feel awkward and manipulated from the beginning.

If you want people to feel included, start as you mean to go on. The most powerful way is to start by some introduction in which everyone says something. Each person speaking, everyone else listening, from the beginning, seems to help people both contribute and listen better throughout. In smaller meetings, everyone can do this together; in huge conferences people can lean over the backs of their fixed seats and spend five minutes introducing themselves. The buzz is amazing – and people are then able to listen and participate better during the meeting.

Can you skip this part in groups that meet regularly? No, says an experienced facilitator, describing the consequences when she moved straight to the business with a group that met weekly. "Usually our meetings were lively; this time it felt like we were all walking through wet cement. At the end, when we did a brief review, they told me how much they had missed our usual 'checking in'. It only took five minutes but everyone felt this time reconnected them

as human beings rather than as functions in a busy department."

Remind and renegotiate
Both the quality of the business and the relationships in a group will benefit if everyone starts with the same information about why they are there. Some people will not have received the agenda in advance of the meetings; some will say they haven't – and many won't have read what they did receive. In addition, there may be newcomers to a long-standing meeting, and any other number of other reasons to remind people of the purpose and programme. As the chair you may wish that everyone had read the agenda: don't assume or blame. Just find an effective way to get everyone to the same place, to achieve the goals of the meeting. Blame is not an effective way of doing that.

Voila!

RIP

After the reminder comes the renegotiation. If the agenda doesn't any longer represent the priorities of the group, you may want to adjust it. One organizer admitted she initially found this idea extremely difficult when the facilitator suggested it: "I had consulted so much in advance and briefed people to prepare presentations for the items on the agenda. Quite frankly I was in tears when the facilitator pointed out that people now wanted to talk about the impact of an

Introduce newcomers
Pay special attention to anyone joining your group for their first meeting.

Remember, there is no such thing as an old group with a new member. Each time someone new attends a meeting, you have a new group.

Transform tardiness
Greet latecomers in a way that neither disrupts the meeting nor communicates hostility. As the chair you might:

- Say hello then continue with the meeting
- Suggest the person get refreshments and settle
- Get a volunteer to brief the latecomer during a break.

If their tardiness becomes a habit, talk to them outside the meeting.

unexpected policy change on their work. But when he insisted and we changed – the life came back into the meeting. And I learnt a big lesson."

By tradition, "any other business" sits at the end of the agenda. In that place it is a saboteur, just waiting to explode a surprise when everyone is tired and ready to finish. Instead, any other business belongs at the beginning of the meeting, when you are checking whether you need to make any changes to the agenda. The negotiations need not be lengthy. But to create a lively and relevant meeting, you need to ensure that the agenda is alive and relevant.

Make judgements about time and timing
Time together is precious. Whatever was or wasn't done in preparation, the timing during a meeting can help anything work out – or get stuck.

Time and timing is the area that is more contentious than almost any other. There are different cultural styles, organizations get into habits about their timekeeping for meetings and individuals often vote with their tardiness.

An experienced chair describes how long it took her to find some creative way of dealing with timekeeping: "I hate it when people come late. I notice that they then are usually disruptive as if they are guilty for being late. I used to be steaming and my body language at least would communicate that clearly. But one day, I stopped the meeting and told them how I felt and asked what we could do. They decided that members who were on time would be willing to catch up latecomers in the break; that I would say hello and welcome them but otherwise not stop proceedings or repeat what they had missed. I certainly found myself feeling both better and more effective once we'd discussed this honestly."

If you are leading a meeting, you need to make a conscious decision about how long to wait for latecomers. It is true that the only

way to start on time is to start on time. But with a small group and a key participant missing, you may want to delay and explain why and say when you intend to start.

Timekeeping has consequences that will have to be dealt with in the meeting. If the meeting starts an hour late you may not be able to complete all the items – or at least within the timing intended.

You may also find that an item that seemed a quick one in fact hits a deep pothole. The skill is to be open with the group about the dilemmas and choices. Every item on an agenda will be of some interest to at least two members of the group – or it should not be on the agenda. Negotiating the timing is negotiating attention to the different interests in the room.

I feel safe because I'm not at the meeting.

In big meetings, the issue is often how to get people back from breaks. One group came up with an innovative solution which they called "sheepdogs". Instead of the chair having to go around and hassle people and feel a bit like a mother hen, before each break a couple of members of each group agreed to shepherd their colleagues back into the meeting. The facilitator observed: "I felt we were sharing responsibility and the whole atmosphere of our meetings changed."

WORK THROUGH THE AGENDA TOGETHER

The chair's job is to lead the group through the agenda as effectively as possible. This requires the chair to find a balance between helping the group do the business and reading the rhythms and messages of the group. Participants also carry responsibility but it is the chair who leads.

You will only surmount the difficulties that can arise in even the simplest of meetings when you believe it is possible for people to work constructively together. If you don't believe this, it won't happen.

"What do you do if the chair is not doing this very well?" is one of the most frequently asked questions when we are talking with people about meetings. Different situations and people will find different answers. The most respectful is to talk with the chair before or after the meeting; the least helpful is to spend all the time moaning to each other.

Create genuine safety

If we want meetings that are real and productive, we need to create an atmosphere where people can share concerns and propose uncomfortable solutions without fear of being punished or ostracized in some way.

This is a challenging request. Many of our clients work in areas of society and areas of the world in which the social and political environment is not safe.

While completing this book, an email came from a colleague who is working in Sudan, reflecting on the dilemma of participants coming in hope yet fearing for their safety: "When we ask people to come to a meeting we are asking them to be ready to change rather than defend or win in terms of their position. We are asking for a level of vulnerability, self-criticism and questioning that requires some level of safety. We are asking people to feel safe enough to change rather than safe enough to avoid change, which is a false safety."

When you are running a meeting you have responsibility not just for the business of the meeting but also for the emotional environment in which you are doing the business. People need to know that they can speak and act in good faith and be confident enough that there will be no damaging or unpleasant consequences. When you are chair or facilitator, participants will look to your example and this will affect how safe they feel it is to participate.

Navigate the content

The agenda is a road map with the route signposted but the weather and the quality of the road and the moods of your travelling companions often come as a surprise.

The basic skill of a chair is to keep reminding people of the signposts as they journey through the agenda. There is a distinct rhythm to this skill.

You are moving on from a previous and different item; people's attention wanders; some will know in great detail the background to the next item, others won't have a clue. A few words reminding people why an item is on the agenda will bring everyone back to the map. Keep the discussion tight when that is possible; open it out to a free-floating discussion when that is necessary; then pull in tightly to some sort of conclusion. Break when you read that the energy is flagging. Know when to pause creatively. You can make more time by dancing with time.

Balance task and group

Whenever you swing too far in any direction, whether it be with the business or the group, you know you have overbalanced. A skilful chair will bring things back into balance.

There may be times when there is a deadline for an item of business that overrides what is going on between people. A client reported how freeing it had been when she as chair had used her authority to keep a group to their task, despite pressure from two strong members of the team.

Use groups skilfully
Avoid doing business in a big group as much as possible. People can more easily feel disconnected and disaffected if they spend too long in a big group. There are many ways to use smaller groups:

- Task (or "breakout") groups to work in more detail on a question or proposal
- A group of three when asking people to do personal review
- Pairs or small groups, to renew energy and bring clarity to a stalled discussion
- Just on our own – to gather thoughts.

Don't be afraid to try out different ways of working with groups.

CAUGHT IN AN UNDERCURRENT

"Two people wanted the agenda changed to talk about tensions in the staff team. I told them that we had a review meeting at the end of the month and I would put these issues on the agenda. But right now, we had 21 young people going out on work experience placements the next week and only 15 placements. That is our task. Let's get on with it."

Whenever a group focuses solely on either the task or their relationships, it is likely to be a signal that something is out of balance. The best way to find out what is going on is to stop and check.

Hold the tensions
Everyone in a meeting will be looking to the chair for the lead in how to handle a difficult situation. The situation might range from someone dominating a discussion to someone speaking with hostility to a colleague during the meeting.

The skill is to hold the tension of the task and the energies of the group. The chair most obviously does this but any participant can play that role, as one person who has done a lot of training in group dynamics reflected: "I am always the one in our meetings to point out that something isn't being said, that the energy has shifted, that body language is giving off loud signals. My colleagues used to raise their eyes and I could hear them thinking, 'Oh no, there she goes again!' but I've gotten more skilful in how I raise things – and they have come to appreciate having meetings that are more honest."

When conflict or criticism persists, the chair needs to be clear with participants how they will deal with it: whether it is time to stop the business and negotiate peace or steer clear of the issue – or arrange to follow it up in a different way at a different time.

Decide on action: record conclusions
The point of any meeting is to reach a conclusion about each item on the agenda. How you reach these conclusions is as important as the conclusions themselves.

A common pitfall in many meetings is lack of clarity about how decisions are going to be made. The critical issue is to be clear about this at the outset. Otherwise you may talk in circles for hours trying to get everyone's agreement. Your ideal may be the consensus where everyone agrees. How long will you go on when it is obvious that on this issue, everyone will not agree? Always have an alternative if your ideal doesn't work.

There is great skill at this stage in leading a group to a decision while ensuring that the decision is genuinely acceptable to everyone. Often an "efficient" meeting covers quickly all the items on an agenda. It is only after the meeting, when people want to reopen the same item again or simply avoid doing what they said, that you realize something is wrong with the process.

The end of any item on the agenda should be a statement of where you have reached. This not only gives a record for your minutes but can bring to a close a wide-ranging or contentious or confusing conversation, giving people a chance to double-check whether they understand and still agree.

The aim is an effective meeting in which conclusions are reached and people feel involved in the process.

FINISH WELL

It is more important to finish the meeting well than to squeeze in one last item on the agenda. The ending marks the completion of a journey the whole group has taken together. It needs to be a time of pulling together the loose ends, signalling what's next, saying goodbye and leaving people free to move on.

Plan for action in the follow through

People have made decisions of some sort, even if it is to bring an item up at the next meeting. At the end of the meeting, you need to conclude with some clarity about what's next – and a double-check that people know what they have promised to do.

In some huge gatherings, turning decisions into action plans occupies a whole day with a complex set of negotiations. In a small team meeting, it may only require a restatement of what is being taken forward. It is a critical part of ending the meeting.

The challenge of making action plans is perhaps greatest in meetings of networks. In a meeting of European campaigning groups, the representatives saw that their actions would be more effective if they coordinated their individual country-based work with each other and with the timetable of European Union meetings. Everyone supported the strategy: the difficulty was getting a volunteer to take the lead in coordinating the follow through. Most were volunteers with other demanding jobs; several were lone workers in a tiny group; everyone felt torn between their heart for the cause and the day-to-day demands in their lives. The meeting ended with a reluctant volunteer.

The point is the same: people need to leave a meeting knowing by name who is doing what. An item left without a name is an item that you are already signalling will not be turned into action.

Leave extra time for loose ends

It takes courage on the part of the chair to stop the flow of discussion in time to deal with any loose ends effectively. Remember: one or more persons in a meeting have a stake in each item on the agenda – if there is not time to address them, then it is crucial to the credibility of the process that you make time to decide what to do about these unaddressed items.

Undercurrents in the meeting can easily surface at the end of the meeting. A friend wrote about an experience she had when the chair ran out of time for her item, an item on race relations, which he had not wanted to include anyway. "He said, 'Can you take us through this in the last two minutes.' I said, 'No, but I can offer to do so in 15 minutes, if people are willing to stay that long.' They were – and in fact I went on for half an hour, they were so interested."

Reflect, appreciate and say goodbye

At the end of the meeting, the whole group benefits by taking some time to reflect briefly on what we have done (not just what we haven't done), what we have learnt from each other and what we appreciate. The style is the chair's to choose: the chair has to believe in the value of reflection and appreciation in order for others to feel comfortable taking part.

Differing contexts, cultural or personal styles will shape how reflection and appreciations are expressed.

Be alert to postscripts

In some ways the trickiest bit of a meeting is just after it has ended formally. It is then that groups of friends may be making arrangements to go have a drink together while others either aren't interested or feel they are not included.

It is also the time when someone who hasn't spoken up in the meeting may say, as they walk out of the door, "I don't agree with what we've decided." As chair, your meeting doesn't end with the formal finish.

Be vigilant about signals that you may need to follow through after the meeting.

Running short of time?
Do two or three items on the agenda at the same time.

- Delegate each item to a subgroup of the meeting
- Ask each group to recommend ways to move forward.

This way you can do in 20 minutes what would otherwise take 60.

RPQ4OX?

Biscuits, please.

MEETINGS IN PRACTICE
A STORY

WHEN CURRENTS AND UNDERCURRENTS ARE THE MAIN AGENDA

An independent consultant who had been helping a small agency with their strategic planning describes a meeting in which achieving healthier currents and undercurrents in the team is the purpose of the meeting.

This was a meeting I knew would be challenging.

In speaking with each individual in advance of the meeting, I had learned that three of the staff group had begun grievance processes against their manager, claiming she was incompetent. The manager had countered by starting disciplinary proceedings against two of the three. Of the two staff members not subject to proceedings, one was highly supportive of the manager and the other was very supportive of the staff group.

An investigation had, rather unhelpfully, found them all to be at fault, and insisted on this mediated meeting to reconcile their differences.

At the start of the meeting I made it clear that the only topic of discussion was whether, and how, we might build a reasonably effective working environment for the team. I also asked whether we were willing to commit to a nuclear-free zone, i.e. that missiles of words and body language would not be lobbed either over or under the table.

I acknowledged the level of hurt that each individual in the room had experienced as the result of other people's actions, but emphasized that we were not there to retrace old ground.

We met off-site in a comfortable, neutral environment with attached gardens. Every time the conversation became heated, angry or tearful, I would suggest a break for individuals to have time with me to explain their concerns more constructively, or on occasions I mediated an agenda between two individuals. Others used the time for a walk.

It was tough. I needed to choose carefully when to allow a conversation to develop, if it seemed likely to lead to fruitful conclusions, and when to simply stop the flow. I needed to be constantly reassuring and valuing people as individuals, recognizing that this was an enormously difficult journey for them.

At the end, we had achieved three things:
• A temporary truce
• A basic framework for working together over the next few months
• A deeper acknowledgement amongst all of us that the situation was completely unsustainable over the long term for one or more of the individuals.

The man who had been most sceptical about the whole process came to me quietly after the meeting, shook my hand, and said, "We got somewhere, didn't we?"

MEETINGS IN PRACTICE
A STORY

THE HIGH-TECH SOLUTION

A facilitator asked by an international network to help them draft a multimedia protocol describes how they were able to involve colleagues on different continents.

It seemed a tall order for a facilitator. I was asked to find a way of organizing a two-day gathering of museum and gallery professionals from three prestigious art galleries in the United States and the United Kingdom. Their aim was to create common standards and protocols for loans of high-tech multimedia art between institutions.

They desperately wanted a product that would enable institutions with very different systems and processes to work together. They wanted the meeting to be creative, to have the capacity to engage with host institutions and to produce, at the end of two days, a working document for which they all felt responsible.

Twenty-five people sitting round a table talking for two days was clearly not going to do it. The question was, what would?

How about, I thought, pretending that we are a virtual media production unit, where groups of people could work together focusing on producing key documents, whilst having the capacity to talk, as required, to other colleagues in the room who would be working on other documents. Where colleagues back in the host institutions could watch progress on web cameras and make comments and suggestions by email. Where the computer networks and databases of host institutions could be consulted live, online. And where I, as facilitator, could act as production manager, editor-in-chief, ringmaster and convenor of planning and editorial meetings.

We needed:
- A basic agenda dividing the work into five main elements
- Five work stations with five people at each, and at each work station:
  - Computer
  - Projector
  - Flip chart
  - Ample space
  - Typist
  - Web camera
  - Internet access and a dedicated email address.

Throughout those two days we all met together periodically, to ensure clarity about the task, to agree general standards, terminology and length of contributions. In between, the five groups produced their texts, which were instantly displayed, both to those in the room and on the Internet. Comments could come in at any time. From time to time, each group presented their work so far and submitted it to scrutiny.

In the midst of the gathering, it felt intense and crazy, but it was an inspirational and wonderfully effective method of working, with a great product by the end of the two days.

CHAPTER 6
INVITE GENUINE COMMUNITY

INVITE GENUINE COMMUNITY
AT A GLANCE

There are many ways to talk about the mysterious territory where an assortment of individuals turn into a community. The following are five active elements that make stepping into such a sense of genuine community more likely:

- Be truthful and trustworthy

- Keep in touch with the purpose and your passions

- Work imaginatively

- Face up to difficult conversations

- Use the power of pauses.

CHAPTER 6
INVITE GENUINE COMMUNITY

As a poet said, "A meeting is not a me-thing, it is a we-thing." Whatever the task, working together is a "we-thing".

The "we-thing" is what we are calling "community". We are using the term "community" in a variety of ways. In the meeting itself, it is the move from disparate people with distracted energy to a focus on the common cause that brought them together.

To aspire to create community in a meeting doesn't mean easy answers or lack of conflict. A colleague was chairing an international network of people gathered from all sides in a civil war in their home country. He reported that "People didn't agree at the end, but we did experience a moment when everyone recognized these were other human beings, behind their labels and all the history. It was very moving."

It takes a sort of changing gears to move from an assortment of people just there to get a job done to a glimpse of the potential of the group and its effect on wider worlds.

The benefits of community in a meeting continue beyond the meeting itself. The wider communities influenced by the outcomes of a meeting can include neighbourhoods, or Internet connections, an organization or a worldwide network.

THINK BACK to a moment in a meeting when you felt things shift gear – when the people came together in their full potential as a community. What for you were ingredients in that shift? What part did you play? What part did you observe others playing? What in the preparation for the meeting contributed to the magic? Did that promise continue afterwards in the follow through?

That moment when something shifts in a meeting is difficult to put into words but we recognize it when we are in it: assorted and diverse people and time and place and business come together in a most unexpected and transforming moment.

The "me-thing" has become a "we-thing". This connection can't be guaranteed. But there are things we can do, or not do, that create the possibility that our work together will touch that something. This connection cannot be put on the agenda but it is the potential behind everything, in any sort of meeting or conference. It is both a deepening in our meeting together – and a lightening up.

In even the smallest and most routine of meetings, we can get a glimpse of an alternative future as we collaborate on something that one person cannot achieve just by themselves.

The shift does not always come from a major upheaval in a meeting or a difficult conversation. A client who organizes many meetings said, "I have seen a whole meeting shift just by moving the tables and chairs into a better arrangement. Don't forget that space in itself can transform our relationships."

BE TRUTHFUL AND TRUSTWORTHY

Ultimately, the real power we each have in a meeting is to be truthful and trustworthy. It is our responsibility to ourselves, to the group and to the task to which we have come with commitment.

A friend of ours teaching at a university cautions about making false promises about safety and trust: "I tell my students in the first class – which is like a meeting – that no one is entirely trustworthy, that they must make their own judgements about how much to share and how to participate, based on that reality. By being honest with them, we can have deeper conversations more quickly."

Being truthful in a meeting can be transforming. One colleague pointed out that this didn't just mean being honest about conflicts in the group. "I was meant to chair a meeting one day and I was unprepared and exhausted. Instead of pretending, I was just honest with the group. It is no surprise that everyone else felt the same way. So we made more space during

the day for pauses, starting with a long walk. And interestingly enough, we got through the agenda as well."

And if you don't feel the setting is safe enough for you to take the risk of speaking up? Being honest with ourselves about that can in itself shift the quality of our involvement.

KEEP IN TOUCH WITH THE PURPOSE AND YOUR PASSIONS

If you are in the midst of a meeting where you are beginning to go to sleep, and are asking, "Why have I bothered to be here?", remind yourself what difference you hoped the meeting would make. If you can rediscover your own corner of curiosity and enthusiasm you can affect the energy in the whole group.

A client described how he finds that rhythm in his management meetings at the hospice he runs: "We can get bogged down in talking about fund-raising or worrying about the accounts. To listen to us we could be any management team for anything. We have learnt to start our meetings now with an update on different patients and their families. That reminds us of the point of balancing the budget."

A meeting is a slice of our time that will not come round again. Part of what motivated us to write this book was the number of colleagues who were yearning for ways to make meetings places where the passions in their lives and their work could be respected and where they could contribute to their common cause.

WORK IMAGINATIVELY

Creativity in a meeting doesn't mean getting everyone to sing and dance the decisions – unless that furthers the decision-making! It means using the widest resources available – in the environment, amongst people and

Record imaginatively
Supplement formal records with alternative ways of telling the story:

- A roving photographer
- A poet in residence
- A cartoonist
- A story teller
- A video record.

Use them during the meeting, in the final summary, and for the final report.

I meet therefore I am

in the variety of materials provided – to address serious issues rather than digging deeper holes. The aim is to liberate the diversity of skills, experience and cultural awareness available to the group.

Over lunch at the end of a three-day conference for 200 staff, the planning group reflected on what had made the experience feel like a bit of magic to them. The organizer summarized: "We knew it wasn't 'perfect' but we were delighted with our work together. This is some of what made it happen, we thought:

- People offering their skills and ideas and talents and taking risks with new things
- Our group planning meticulously then being flexible during the conference
- The space for more imaginative activities, for example the writing, the office displays, the poems, the magic trick with the flags of different countries
- Laughter (in every large session)
- Our support for each other
- Delegating a lot
- The flow: we got the rhythm right!"

When people tap into more of their own resources – logic, imagination, perceptions and evidence – the solutions will seem simple because they have come from the whole range of resources we have available to us as human beings. Although we often limit ourselves in meetings, we don't have to.

FACE UP TO DIFFICULT CONVERSATIONS

Difficult conversations can be about anything – from a conflict over a budget to differences about religious and political beliefs. We may each approach a meeting with good intent and yet find it difficult to talk honestly with another person or contribute to conversations about the difficulties amongst those present in the room.

To face discomfort and conflict in a group is risky; it is even riskier to totally ignore the undercurrents. Ignored, they seldom go away. It is best to face up to undercurrents

You don't want to be there?
Find one reason that makes it worth staying, even if it is nothing to do with the formal purpose of the meeting. Or leave.

Take a risk
Are there talents, interests and skills you use outside work but never with colleagues? Take a chance on using them to enhance your meetings.

I am therefore I meet

sooner rather than later, before the situation either escalates into a major conflict or, alternatively, feels so clamped down that no real conversations can take place.

As a participant, you have an equal responsibility to say what you see and feel if you want the group under the chair's leadership to work more honestly and effectively. People usually find it liberating to have the whole issue named honestly, explored and resolved.

A client described the unexpected effect she had in a meeting. "Two of my colleagues were really having a nasty go at each other, while the rest of us sat there embarrassed and mute. I found myself standing up and almost shouting at them, 'I cannot stand listening to you talk to each other like this.' Everyone stopped in stunned silence. The atmosphere changed and settled. And they apologized."

THE POWER
OF
PAUSES

Remember first to talk with someone and then about something. When something is going off course in a group, the chair needs to find ways to help people have conversations with each other that reconnect them. It is in such conversations that the gem of genuine community lies hidden. One facilitator shares his approach to serious conflict: "I sometimes ask those in most

obvious conflict to talk together during a break, sometimes with my help, then make a shared presentation to the group. I tell them they do not have to agree on the points, simply present their disagreements together. It has a profound effect."

USE THE POWER OF PAUSES

Often the habit in meetings is to keep going, a bit like holding your breath in a school race as you run to the finish line. Yet the greatest untapped power in any meeting is in the pauses.

We have learnt that there is usually a stage in dealing with a challenging agenda item where things look pretty negative and hopeless. Don't be afraid to pause. It is the chair's responsibility to reflect on what a pause might be about or might achieve. First of all, the chair needs to ask whether they are avoiding a difficult issue or conflict. The chair may need to take a quick mental pause to reflect on whether a pause for the whole group will help, hinder or exacerbate the issue under discussion.

If you feel an undercurrent in a group, it is important to stop and check out what is going on rather than assume the worst. Sometimes discomfort in a group is nothing more serious than the central heating or hunger pangs. Check, don't assume.

A colleague reflected on how pauses can transform a meeting into a community. "Inviting genuine community is difficult. If I'm in a meeting, in whatever role, I am part of the same dynamic as everyone else. So at some point in the proceedings I may feel confused or lost or uncomfortable. This is a potentially powerful moment. To know what to do, I may need some time to think. That's when I need a pause."

A pause can offer the chance to slow things down, cool it for a little while, so we can reconnect with ourselves and others. Community is that connection. We can invite it but not command it to transform our meetings. That is the potential in any meeting, if we invite it in.

Speak up – non-violently
How can we speak up honestly and passionately but without sarcasm, hostility or harm? Try avoiding judgements and opinions. Instead:

- Give information or facts so everyone knows what you are referring to
- Say how you feel about what is happening
- Be clear about what you want to change.

Abandon the label "problem" and notice how much more open the discussion becomes.

THE MEETING CONTINUUM
AFTER THE MEETING
40%

After the meeting comes the full proof of its value. We are asking, what is different because we met? What are we going to do to take forward our intentions?
And what can we learn?

The final stage of The Meeting Continuum offers two systematic ways of looking at what emerged from the meeting:

CHAPTER 7
FOLLOW THROUGH
The real end of the meeting happens after the formal finish. This is also the beginning of action on the promises we made during the meeting as we weave them into the wider context of our lives.

CHAPTER 8
REFLECT AND LEARN
After the meeting we have opportunities to stand back and see what we have learnt about ourselves and our group and what we want to do about that.

The energy from a good meeting helps you to sustain intentions afterwards.

CHAPTER 7
FOLLOW THROUGH

FOLLOW THROUGH
AT A GLANCE

To sustain the work and the relationships from the meeting,
we can take the following steps after the meeting:

COMPLETE THE BUSINESS OF THE MEETING
- Complete unfinished business
- Debrief appropriately
- Communicate widely and well

ACKNOWLEDGE WHAT IS CHANGING AS A RESULT OF THE MEETING
- Spot unexpected issues emerging
- Identify changes for you
- Be honest about changes for someone else
- Beware of too much change, too little transition

DO WHAT YOU SAID YOU WERE GOING TO DO
- Continue your role as the chair
- Fulfil your responsibilities as participants.

CHAPTER 7
FOLLOW THROUGH

Follow through is probably the most neglected stage of a meeting and yet it is the one on which the credibility of the meeting rests. It is after a meeting that you show whether the work you discussed is sustainable and you see how widely the influence of the meeting will be felt.

At this stage moving your ideas and intentions into reality is the final creative challenge in The Meeting Continuum.

Think of any meeting like a boat that has set its sails in a particular direction. The obvious consequences of the meeting have set you on course or readjusted it; but the waves that you create as you sail towards your destination can fan out in unexpected directions with unexpected consequences. At this third stage in The Meeting Continuum, you need to look more widely than straight ahead.

At the beginning of the continuum we have looked imaginatively and rigorously at how to work together; in the second stage we have brought these creative ideas to the meeting itself. The final and equally powerful stage is the follow through.

THINK BACK to a meeting you attended a month or so ago. Can you remember what came out of the meeting? What had you promised to take forward? Have you? Decide what one step you need to take to be more effective after a meeting.

For some of us, this stage of completing something is more difficult than for others. One director of a large organization commented with some surprise, after being introduced to The Meeting Continuum and its 40:20:40 pattern: "I never really thought about follow through before. I suspect that is why so few decisions get put into practice and why my staff are so disgruntled with my leadership. It just never occurred to me; I'm better on the big ideas, and I am always so relieved to have the meeting over with."

Sometimes a whole team will be lacking in someone who wants to pin down the practical next steps. That is why it is important to identify and name who has the responsibility for coordinating the different aspects of the follow through discussed below.

You will need to adapt these aspects of follow through to suit the style and needs of the people you are working with. As with preparation, the time all this takes will decrease as you become more practised at follow through and less inclined to procrastinate.

I'm following you.

COMPLETE THE BUSINESS OF THE MEETING

Few meetings are completed when the finish time has come and gone. Some unfinished business may need to be done within hours of the formal end to the meeting, such as debriefing with a planning group; others at least within the week afterwards, such as communicating the consequences of the meeting.

Complete unfinished business

Unfinished business will block effective follow through.

There is likely to be something in the meeting that didn't quite get completed. Sometimes this is recognized and noted at the end of the meeting; sometimes it only becomes clear in writing up the meeting or making your plan of action. Each item not dealt with on the agenda has behind it one or more people for whom it was of some importance. If you did not acknowledge such items at the end of the meeting and agree how and when to take them forward, you need to do so now.

Often people leave a meeting with a bad taste about an encounter they had with someone else in the meeting. They are more likely to grumble about it to a trusted individual than deal with it openly; when this happens, the undercurrent can become toxic and dangerous to the wider group. The more quickly this disaffection can be faced, the less likely the feelings are to spill over into everyday work and affect others too.

To deal with such undercurrents may require a great deal of personal courage in being open with someone you normally would not speak with in such a way. The youngest member of a small planning group felt that the chair had slighted her quite publicly and obviously, whether it was intentional or not. She raised this after the meeting with the chair, explaining, "I didn't do so in the meeting because it seemed more important for us to get on with the business. But I knew I had to raise it with

you afterwards if we were to be able to continue working together." The chair thanked her for her honesty.

The principle is that attending to unfinished business quickly will allow everyone to move on.

Debrief appropriately

It is important to take time immediately to capture loose ends and lessons.

For a regular and brief meeting, this debriefing may be simply to check with the note taker that they have the information they need to complete the minutes. If you have chaired the meeting, make your own notes about what you noticed in the group or with the agenda.

For longer and certainly for larger gatherings, a number of people will have been involved in making a meeting happen: the event organizer, facilitators (both from outside and within the group), colleagues

Sooner the better
Getting notes of the meeting out within a week is OK, within 48 hours is good, within 24 hours is brilliant. Notes arriving soon after the meeting will be energizing. Getting them after a week drains energy.

ACKNOWLEDGE WHAT IS CHANGING AS A RESULT OF THE MEETING

Consider your meeting like a stone thrown into a lake. The ripples are more distinct at first, then subtly ripple out and down, merging with the greater body of water. So with the consequences of the meeting.

We go into a meeting with some sense that we will be changing something – whether it is our ideas, a way of working on a project or the priorities we place on different aspects of our work and working lives. Some of these we might have predicted; others emerge during the meeting itself.

One of the early tasks of the follow through stage of The Meeting Continuum is to stop and assess the implications and impact of the meeting as widely as possible.

Name names

Know who is accountable for any promise. That way you can check with them – or refer people to them (and know who is going to check in and check up on progress).

who took lead roles, a planning group. A conversation with them, whether at the end of the meeting or in the week or so afterwards, will give information for use in planning the follow through and preparing for future meetings. Do this face to face if you can, by phone or video conference or even email if people are spread out.

Communicate widely and well

How can we communicate skilfully? Each person attending a meeting is often representing the interests and work of many others, whether officially or unofficially. Those being represented need to hear what impact the meeting might have on their own work.

Communicate in a style that suits what you have to say and who needs to hear it, for example:
- A record of decisions, which becomes the legal record once signed
- A prompt for action for those at the meeting
- A newsletter item or emailed briefing memo for those who did not attend
- Key messages conveyed to those who need them
- Phone calls or direct conversations, not emails, to those who were absent.

Spot unexpected issues emerging

In almost any meeting, there is the business on the agenda and then there are wider or deeper issues that are often not recognized or voiced. After one meeting a participant acknowledged that the plans they had just made were totally unrealistic. "Everyone knew this during the meeting but we were afraid to challenge the chief executive's enthusiasm. Our consultations in our teams after the meeting began to reveal the realities and it became clear that we would have to discuss the subject again."

When we were talking about the responsibility of each participant to follow through on their promises, a colleague involved in many international conferences on human rights and disaster relief wrote reflecting on his experience: "Sometimes during the meeting there is a sense that a shift in understanding has been achieved. Yet maybe it had failed to recognize that undercurrents still abounded. It is also often the case that a decision is not the end of the matter – repercussions may not have been obvious at the time, the desire of participants to reach agreement had masked their true feelings, certain factions had acquiesced for now but still intended to regroup (sometimes quite rightly, if a powerful faction had overridden their concerns at the time)."

Identify changes for you

Any meeting will have consequences for each person who attended. Ask yourself:

- What am I having to readjust as a consequence of commitments I made at the meeting?
- What do I need to do more of?
- What therefore will I need to do less of?

You are likely to need to talk with others in your team or group to find the answers.

Be honest about changes for someone else

Often the decisions in meetings have consequences for others who were not at the meeting. Great ideas require a lot of administrative support. One secretary in a school complained, "Every time they have a big idea, we end up with a huge amount of work and no more resources. They seem to manage to get extra staff themselves but never remember the consequences on typing and accounting and filing."

Beware of too much change, too little transition

Having a great idea is one thing; helping everyone to make the changes required to make it happen is another thing entirely.

An experience with one large organization in the midst of a big organizational change highlights the tension between a great new idea and the capacity to make it happen. The consultant for the annual days away as a management group described what happened. "The 20 middle managers who were meant to give the lead to the changes were simply not participating in discussions about all these changes. Whatever we tried, they didn't come to life. Finally, we stopped, took them aside from the senior management team, and asked what was going on.

"Several were almost in tears. They said they felt they were carrying the whole burden of the change – the expectations of the seniors, the fears of the juniors – while doing their own old jobs at the same time as planning for a new way of working. Some admitted to drinking more at lunchtime, others to finding themselves sleepless and angry at home. The result? The next session, with all the managers, I got them to take a practical look at the realities: the results? A slowing down of the pace of the transition, not its ultimate goal; additional practical support to the managers; a monthly review of progress and concerns; extra administrative resources in the short term. And a sigh of relief."

DO WHAT YOU SAID YOU WERE GOING TO DO

The credibility of the meeting is affected by the behaviour of the chair and the participants after the meeting. Do what you said you would do – or signal quickly if you cannot. Treat colleagues who were not at the meeting with the clarity and respect you fostered in the meeting itself.

Don't leave it to chance
The success of the meeting depends on people doing what they said. Put a note in your diary right now to check in a month – with yourself and others – that the main things resulting from the meeting have been done.

READY TO GO FORWARD

Report back, feedback
Bring the meeting to life
for colleagues by:

- Sharing highlights
- Summarizing issues
  that affect them
- Feeding back their
  responses.

This two-way traffic of
reporting and responding
is crucial for maintaining
healthy communities and
organizations.

Continue your role as the chair
If you are the chair of these meetings, you
will carry on with that role, as, for example,
did a person who chaired the board of
trustees of one national organization. She
described how she sees her role between
meetings: "You need to think of the board
as an ongoing board, not just people
showing up for meetings. The board
members need maintenance between
meetings. For example, we are now in the
midst of a structural review. So each time
I meet with the consultant who is leading
on the review, I email all the board members.
When I go on visits to our various projects,
I email them to tell them what I've observed.
I am very busy as the chair between
meetings!"

As chair, if you created an environment
of respect in working together, you have
implied or promised that people would be
listened to and not attacked or punished for
speaking truthfully. It is important that you
follow this through after the meeting, to the
best of your ability.

Fulfil your responsibilities as participants
If you are involved in making the decisions
in a meeting, you have committed yourself
to representing those decisions back to
your own constituency. The decision may
not be the one for which you were lobbying
but if you have said, by the end of the
meeting, at the least, "I or we can live with
this", then you have made a promise to
take this decision back to your group –
and to feed back to your chair if somehow
this intention will not work in practice.

Often the greatest gap in follow through
is described by those who did not
attend yet whose work is affected by the
decisions of the meeting: "We were never
given information about what happened
at the meeting." Each participant has
a responsibility to tell others.

Of course follow through generates meetings
of its own, whether these are significant
conversations with one other person or
a meeting of a group whose work has
changed as a result of the initial meeting.
And so The Meeting Continuum continues.

MEETINGS IN PRACTICE
AN EXAMPLE

What happened? Recording and communicating

There are a number of ways you can record and communicate what happened at the meeting. Think carefully both about what you want to say and also about how different people can best receive the information. Here are four different ways of recording and communicating an agenda item on workforce diversity, designed for different audiences.

FORMAL MINUTES FOR A LEGAL RECORD

Senior Management Team, 5 March 2006, London
Attended: Peter Gerson, Ahmed Basrat, Daksha Persad. Apology: Hildegard Adams

Item 1. Recruitment/retention: Building a diverse workforce
The report from our human resources director was considered. It was agreed:
1. That we should seek to ensure that within two years the make-up of the staff group should more accurately reflect the diverse population we serve.
2. That we should immediately contract with an external consultant to review and help us implement changes in recruitment, selection and retention.

ACTION MINUTES FOR THOSE IN THE MEETING

Item 1. Diversity: We aim to ensure we develop a diverse workforce
1. Recruit external consultant: AB by 14.4.06
2. Form internal task force: PG by 10.5.06
3. Prepare budget: GC by 1.4.06
4. Update managers' conference: HA by 8.6.06
5. Prepare briefing notes for all staff: PG by 6.3.06

ITEM IN STAFF NEWSLETTER

Diversity: Recruitment and retention
We are getting some help to see how we can match our staff group to the people we are working with. Alice in human resources is going to recruit a consultant to help us. Watch this space for updates.

BRIEFING NOTES AS A MEMO TO ALL STAFF

Circulation to: All staff
Method of circulation: Email
From a meeting of the Senior Management Team, 5 March 2006.

Item 1. Diversity: Recruitment and retention
The SMT committed the organization to ensuring we develop a diverse workforce that reflects the client group we serve.

We agreed to employ consultants to review and implement changes in our policies on recruitment, selection and retention. Please let Hildegard Adams know if you would like to participate in the working group advising the consultant.

MEETINGS IN PRACTICE
A STORY

SAME INTENTION: DIFFERENT CONCLUSIONS

Here are stories of two organizations with the same intention in their plans – and very different conclusions in the follow through.

Both agencies have long and strong cultures of meticulous planning. Their clients are becoming more diverse in gender, age, language, and national and ethnic background. In both organizations the decision was taken at a senior level to increase the diversity of the staff to meet the increasing diversity of the clients.

For the first agency this same decision has been recorded in minutes of strategic reviews for the senior team every year for the past five years. In most years there has been no plan for following through on this decision: on the occasion when there was a follow through plan, the decision was not acted upon because there was no one designated to make sure something happened. The commitment to creating a more diverse staff is in reality an accumulation of action plans at the back of someone's filing cabinet.

The second agency had the same experience of clients from more diverse backgrounds and the staff group not representative of the general population of the clients they serve. Their senior management team took a decision to ensure that the make-up of the staff group should more accurately reflect the diverse population of clients.

The senior staff in this organization then set about looking for ways to implement the decision. The chief executive officer took on the role as champion of this commitment, with the head of human resources as the person named to take the practical lead. A task group was set up under the leadership of the chief executive officer, with the head of personnel to give practical support. They contracted with an external consultant-evaluator to help them implement this decision in the organization and reflect on their own work and attitudes. The group considered practical options in recruitment, selection, and supporting new staff who come into the agency.

What factors might account for these differences? The intention to change is only one stage in the process of change and is voiced usually by a minority to begin with. There also needs to be a readiness to change; collective reflection and awareness of the issues both in principle and as they affect everyone; and an ownership of the intention by the majority of staff, not just the management. There needs to be willingness to commit to transformation and a profound and practical understanding of the difference between a process of change that is truly transformative and one that is merely dramatic or cosmetic.

Follow through is therefore dependent on the meticulous and thorough processing of these preceding stages. In the case of the first agency, this clearly did not happen; in the second agency, the intention was more collectively owned and understood.

There isn't a magical happily-ever-after ending to the story: Five years later little has changed in the first agency. The second one has struggled with the complex issues arising from their decision. The implementation of that single decision, to actively encourage a more diverse staff, generated hundreds of hours of time across the organization. Yet a great deal of change is evident and the chief executive officer, with his personnel staff, continues to introduce new staff to the principles of the commitment and review it annually.

MEETINGS IN PRACTICE
A STORY

CHANGING AN ENTIRE ORGANIZATION'S CULTURE OF MEETINGS

Here is the story of one international aid agency that finally faced the cost of its culture of meetings and other communication. An audit revealed these aspects of its meetings culture:

- Deep commitment amongst all staff to the purpose of the agency, which was to serve some of the world's poorest people
- An expectation that everyone had to be involved in all meetings
- Staff spending close to 60-70% of their time in meetings, often unproductively
- Little clarity about who actually could make decisions
- Chronic frustration, sometimes turning into a culture of blame that became both personal and prejudiced, contrary to all the organization's values, for example "He's from X and they are authoritarian; she is Y and never on time"
- So much time spent in meetings meant that people were doing their work at home, with resulting overload, and a toxic undertow of complaining in a highly principled agency.

For example, the agency would agonize over whether they could afford to give a grant of £10,000 to a project in a particular developing country while not realizing that one ineffective one-day meeting, with 40 people attending, would cost that same amount.

Hard as it was, the organization faced up to the seriousness of the situation, recognizing that its purpose and values were being undermined by the culture of its communications, especially in meetings. It undertook an honest audit of the purpose, quantity, quality and creativity of its meetings and decision-making culture. These were some of the outcomes:

- The purpose and brief of each meeting were clarified, including who should be attending and how they would communicate their work to others.
- Responsibility for making decisions was delegated to smaller units in the organization.
- Each meeting was set in the context of a particular project and was the responsibility of that project's management.
- With roles and responsibilities suddenly clearer, the need to consult – or not – was more carefully defined.

The organization faced the fact that chairing meetings is as important and distinctive a skill as managing a budget or supervising a member of staff. They moved away from the "anyone can do it" habit by:

- Creating a list of those staff with skills to chair (and not all of these were senior in the organization)
- Training those on the list in running much more focused meetings
- Budgeting time in meetings as scrupulously as budgeting for any other resource.

The result of this was that time spent in meetings dropped from 60-70% to closer to 20%.

There were wider repercussions, of course, as there always are with any change. In order to balance the tighter structure of meetings, people were encouraged to keep talking with each other but in different and less formal ways. The layout of offices was rearranged so that different departments met in the course of their work and shared the same kitchen.

After a couple years, however, staff needs and external circumstances had changed and it was time to review again.

CHAPTER 8
REFLECT AND LEARN

Now - water
the plant.

REFLECT AND LEARN
AT A GLANCE

At this final stage of The Meeting Continuum, you may want to reflect on your learning in a variety of ways:

- **Review the process of the meeting**

- **Learn as an organization**

- **Challenge yourself**

- **Change into new habits**

- **Remember to celebrate.**

CHAPTER 8
REFLECT AND LEARN

The intensity of a meeting is like a spotlight on your normal everyday life; it shows up things you may not normally see or want to see. Any meeting therefore offers rich opportunities for learning about yourself and your wider community.

At this final step in The Meeting Continuum we need to stand back and reflect. Such pauses will give us the practical and emotional information not just about that particular meeting but about what is going on more widely – and then the choice about what we want to do about that information.

I find I get the most done when I hold a meeting of one with myself.

THINK BACK to the meeting you recently found most challenging. What kind of reflecting did you do? With whom? What changes have you made as a result, either individually or with the group? What has helped you to take steps that might transform the next meeting? What has blocked you from doing so?

There are both organizational and individual benefits from taking time to reflect and learn.

REVIEW THE PROCESS OF THE MEETING

The challenge after any meeting is how to take forward both the business and the learning from the meeting. One of the most successful innovations we have seen recently has been with a national organization where the 200 staff meet together quarterly. Cynics said about past all-day meetings that nothing ever happened with all their ideas and proposals. The planning group for the latest all-staff day took on as a challenge how to make the day relevant to their work:

- At the end of a day of discussions, each participant made notes to themselves on a postcard of the issues that might affect their work and saved this to take to their next team meeting.
- Within the month after the staff day, a meeting was scheduled in every team in the organization, including the senior management team. Each team worked to a common agenda: planning into their work schedule any practical outcomes of the staff day, and reviewing the day and making recommendations for the next one.

As one of the evaluation comments said, "Even the cynics saw that what we achieved on the day made a practical difference to our teams – finally."

This process of review need not be a big deal; it just requires the intention and a bit of time. As with the whole process of The Meeting Continuum, the more you do this, the easier and quicker it becomes.

LEARN AS AN ORGANIZATION

Most organizations would say they aspire to be a "learning organization". A learning organization is one that reflects, learns – and then makes changes that will bring principles, intentions and actions into a closer alignment.

Meetings reveal aspects of the wider community or organizational culture. Just by observing yourself and others in a meeting, you will be in a better position to understand the wider context. For instance, meetings offer useful insights into how to best manage the kind of change your group is aiming for. A meeting can reveal any of these aspects of your group:

- The level of common cause, connection and support that exists in the group
- The organizational culture that affects how you do business together
- What you do very well – and may be forgetting to acknowledge
- Where you are stuck as a group
- The levels of stress and commitment.

In seeing meetings as reflections, you may also see the need to change some organizational habits, which are what we call its culture. A new chief executive

reflected on the need for a culture change in her own organization's meetings: "It was a very good organization but with some traditions that were blocking its growth. I was brought in to change the organization and bring it into the 21st century: without new blood, I can't do that – and the new ones will leave unless they know that they are taken seriously. And it's our meetings that undermine this. The old guard speaks at length and ignores or discourages contributions from newer colleagues." A year later, she had started the cultural change by ensuring that team leaders were encouraged to run their own team meetings more imaginatively. She also formed a planning group of old and new staff together to plan their big public events.

CHALLENGE YOURSELF

A meeting offers you the opportunity to strengthen your own best contributions and step back from those habits that are undermining you.

Don't underestimate the power of a group for both good and ill. Ultimately each of us is responsible for our own personal survival and for acting from our own personal awareness, whatever the circumstances. Each person who takes part in a meeting helps or hinders progress towards working together in an effective and challenging community.

You will regain a sense of your own power when you start thinking about either moving into a situation to contribute to change or moving out. You may want to:

- Consider what you contribute and where you feel less than comfortable with your own behaviour
- Decide who could support you practically to develop in the ways you intend
- Make conscious choices for yourself.

Usually people choose to have some individual support to make such changes, or to go on a training course. One chief executive we know undertook some very public personal development. "I wasn't

Pause once a year
Schedule an annual review for any meeting of any sort.

Ask:
- Do we all know why we are meeting?
- Is the membership of the group still appropriate?
- Do the arrangements still work?
- What have we achieved this past year?
- What are our goals for next year?

Keep what is working, change what is not.

Don't let any meetings keep going just because they always have.

satisfied with how I chaired the meetings of my senior management team and I could tell the others weren't either. When finally I asked one colleague directly, he told me honestly how ineffective I was in chairing our meetings. I was recommended a mentor who helped me personally but I also got him to sit in on our meetings for six months and observe how we were working together. He gave me public feedback during the meeting and led discussions with the whole group. I am astonished at how much we get done now – and how much we enjoy meeting together. I am also astonished in retrospect at how I had been promoted to chief executive without any training – or feedback – in running meetings which, after all, are a huge part of my job."

Meetings are groups whose behaviour may trigger previous traumas. A bad experience with a group may leave you with a fear of future meetings. A refugee and community worker who had the experience of a re-education camp in his own country told

us, "I have found it really difficult to be open in meetings in the Western style of speaking up because our whole experience in the re-education camps was of meetings used to attack and humiliate us in public." Recognizing this vulnerability, he has worked in his organization to design, run and write about ways of meeting that practise the value of mutual respect.

CHANGE INTO NEW HABITS
The very act of giving attention to your meetings will probably have highlighted and polished up the strengths in your group and begun the organic process of shedding some of those habits you identified as less helpful. Taking action on the result of a personal or organizational review isn't as simple as talking about it. Don't try to change everything all at once. Start with what is easiest or most urgent or simply what you have the authority to do.

You may choose, for instance, to test out more creative approaches in one meeting for which you have responsibility even if you are in an organization that is not yet ready to move comprehensively towards a healthier culture of meetings.

Both the chair and the chief executive of one organization with a governing body of 75 people recognized that an overhaul of their whole structure of governance was needed. They also knew they could not do all this immediately: too many other changes were more immediate. Four times a year the trustees met together with everyone facing each other all day in banked fixed seats in meetings that were, to quote one frank member, "dire". As the chair reflected, "Changing the whole governance structure was a long-term proposition. But I knew if I failed to act at all on the feedback about the frustration with our meetings, disillusion would grow. So I simply changed the seating! People sat at tables of eight; I got them to discuss agenda items in these smaller groups before contributing to the wider group. Of course it is crazy to work with a group of 75 as a governing body, but in the short

I couldn't get a word in...

term, the quality of our meetings has changed dramatically – and I suspect that will give us the mandate to go ahead with other changes."

Remember, all of us have some stake in the old habits that are familiar. To build on the strengths in ourselves and our group, we need to negotiate and navigate.

A consultant colleague reported back on a session she led with an organization to review the quality and quantity of their meetings: "We had endless pieces of paper with all these good ideas when I interrupted them and said, 'You obviously know what you need to do to make your meetings better. Why don't you?'

"Then we had the significant conversation we had all been avoiding. They described their reluctance to try something new in front of others in their team, for fear of making a mess of it. Some of them described bad experiences in meetings with senior managers and felt those most senior were not committed to changing their own behaviour in meetings. One person summed up what most were feeling: 'We don't have the time for all these things we've suggested and after all, they are just meetings, aren't they?'"

We realized that most people had not yet understood the effect of toxic meetings on their personal and organizational health or the power and responsibility each person had in a meeting. That is why we have offered in *Meeting Together* different ways of thinking about meetings as well as practical ways of making better meetings.

Assume that habits don't change immediately – so don't give up.

REMEMBER TO CELEBRATE
Meetings put us on the spot.

The way to come through the process of meetings feeling good in any circumstances is to celebrate our intentions, our small steps, and our willingness to learn.

So often meetings have an element of trauma as people try to resolve conflicts, yet leave with a sense of failure as they realize they haven't achieved all they set out to. It is important, therefore, to acknowledge and celebrate those successes that have been achieved.

Celebration and meetings are not usually perceived as the most obvious companions. Yet even in situations of enormous tension and open conflict, it is possible to honour the journey shared, the risks taken and the moments of possibility. A friend who often

facilitates meetings amongst people whose communities are in devastating situations described what he has learned: "We have tried all sorts of ways to lighten our meetings while respecting the seriousness of our task. I have found that music and eating together works for us every time. In many traditions, however great the grief, hospitality is offered. It feels important that we do that with our meetings. We need to celebrate that whatever the practical outcome, we have met together."

"Reflect and learn" marks the end of The Meeting Continuum for the meeting or series of meetings that you have been thinking about. You will have changed your world in some way by the attention to the heart and craft of the meeting and will be ready to begin again along The Meeting Continuum from a different place.

Celebrate
Find ways to appreciate your work together. Figure out what would feel appropriate to at least the majority of your group.

Think about:
- The cost: who pays?
- The culture: abseiling or opera, karaoke or ice skating?
- The timing: lunchtime or evenings?

If the intention is to include everyone in celebrations, you will need to consult as meticulously as you would for any other "meeting"!

POSTSCRIPT
REFLECTING FORWARD

Fast forward 20 years or so. Our speculation is that anywhere we look, we will find situations that are more complex and more difficult than those we find so challenging at present. In meetings we are likely to use tools and techniques that we can barely imagine.

Yet this advanced technology will have the same limitation as the technology we can use right now in meetings. The authors firmly believe that the only deep, healing and sustaining answer is individuals meeting with individuals, heart to heart – simple, yet the most complex challenge we have.

FURTHER
INFORMATION
END OF BOOK

ABOUT THE
PUBLISHERS

PLANNING TOGETHER ASSOCIATES

Planning Together Associates is a specialist voluntary and public sector management consultancy whose principal partners are George Gawlinski and Lois Graessle. Their primary focus has been helping chief executives, senior management teams and trustees to plan for and handle organizational change.

They specialize in designing and facilitating meetings and conferences nationally and internationally where a premium is being placed on full participation and clear outcomes. They have considerable experience of working with people from different cultures, faiths, languages and ethnic backgrounds. Over the past 25 years they have undertaken major work with some leading UK voluntary organizations as well as international non-governmental organizations, including in Central and Eastern Europe. They bring this accumulating experience to new agencies.

George Gawlinski has a professional background in social work management. He has worked as an independent organizational consultant for 15 years. He is a visiting lecturer at the University of East Anglia and University College London. He lives and works from his home by the coast in north-west Norfolk, where he indulges his twin passions of family life and sailing.

Lois Graessle has a professional background in journalism, work with young people and managing diverse projects. She has worked as an independent organizational consultant for 25 years. Lois is also a writer and book artist exhibiting her one-off handmade books with Open Books Inc. She lives by rivers in London and Derbyshire.
See www.planningtogether.com.

GET2THEPOINT

Get2thepoint is both a name and a way of getting things done. Martin Farrell had been working independently for three years when he named his new company "get2thepoint". It neatly describes how he goes about helping people to think clearly and act powerfully for the people they care about.

There's an imperative in it. Don't mess about – get to the point. Plan and work together to do your bit to make the world a better place. Get2thepoint works locally, globally and everything in between – small projects, big projects, from a single day to a few months or more, with individuals, groups and organizations.

Most of the time people are not on their own, they're planning and working with other people. So that's where Martin spends much of his time – transforming meetings that once were frustrating and tedious into rich environments to help people think about what they're doing and to get on and do it. These might be team or trustee away days, conferences, coaching one to one or in small groups, or kick-starting projects to get them going.

Get2thepoint is light on its feet, working alongside partners as the opportunity arises – like working with Planning Together Associates to publish this book.
See www.get2thepoint.org.

APPRECIATIONS

We would like to thank organizations with whom we have worked for a number of years; our work together has shown us both the need for a new way of looking at meeting together and the opportunity to create with them special meetings.

Our organizational clients have included:
Amnesty International
Association of Chief Executives of Voluntary Organizations
BBC Children in Need
British Red Cross Society
Christian Aid
Churches Conservation Trust
Directing Change Group
European Council on Refugees and Exiles
General Teaching Council for England
Historic Royal Palaces
International PEN for writers
Jamyang Buddhist Centre
Jersey Heritage Trust
Karim Rida Said Foundation
London Transport Museum
Macmillan Cancer Support
Media Matters
    New Art Trust, Museum of Modern Art,
    San Francisco Museum of Modern Art, Tate Modern
Mental Health Foundation
Mental Health Media
National Society for Epilepsy
North London Hospice
Refugee Action
Rethink Severe Mental Illness
Revolving Doors Agency
Royal Institute of Public Administration
Sainsbury Centre at the University of East Anglia
Scottish Council for Voluntary Organizations
Scottish Refugee Council
Shelter
Stonham Housing Association
Teachers Support Network
Tufts University – United Nations High Commission for Refugees Reconciliation Project
Universal Compassion and Wisdom for Peace
WaterAid
Woodbroke Quaker Study Centre

We have used quotes and examples from our work with these organizations without giving names. Where an organization can easily be identified, we have sought permission from the person who was the chief executive at the time.

ACKNOWLEDGEMENTS

This book itself has been a collaborative effort throughout.

Allan Leas of the European Council on Refugees and Exiles encouraged us to embark on this project when we were in Moscow facilitating a conference of small agencies from Russia, Moldova, Belarus, and Ukraine. Madeline Hutchings of Services for Arts Managers early on invited us to test out our emerging approach with a group of workers in arts organizations. With Simon Keyes of St Ethelburga's Centre for Reconciliation and Peace we piloted our approach in their training for practical peace building. Over many years Sandy Buchan and the staff of Refugee Action have encouraged and inspired us.

We are especially grateful to Rebecca Dale, Dina Glouberman, Alison Murdoch, Nimisha Patel, Chrisitine Wood and Piers Worth, who have commented on drafts at key points and Jackie Parfitt and Natasha Acres at WOW! Creative for their early design input. The book has benefited from the skills and support in our families. Our partners have contributed their skills: Eric Bourne with his eye for grammar and clarity; Lucy Faulkner with her perspective and her story writing. Alexcia Olin Graessle and Julie Thacker Graessle read early drafts. Mark Gawlinski brought his enthusiasm and his editing skills to this project.

We would also like to thank others for their comments and their stories: Lyn Adams, Marieke Bosman, Diana Carroll, Robin Daniels, Jenny Edwards, Harold Garrett-Goodyear, Micki Hobson, Rashid Iqbal, Tanya Kolchanova, Jon Lane, the late Sheila McKechnie, Doreen Massey, Patrick Nash, Carrie Osborne, the late James P. O'Neil, Hyacinth Parsons, Christine Rose, Ann Rose, Philip Rudge, Tricia Sharpe, Holly Stocking, Lilla Tan, Jenny Teuten, Stephen Turner, Van Ly Ung, Deirdre Vereker and Jan Wheatcroft. We have also had conversations, support and encouragement from many others. Thank you.

The late Buntie Wills, artist, town planner and mentor, long ago gave advice, "Talk with someone and only then about something", which kept bringing us back to the heart of the matter. We were delighted to discover the poet Ralph Hoyte whose poem, quoted in Chapter 6, reminds us that meetings are we-things.

Our work on the book also owes a great deal to the walks that we ourselves recommend to clients during many meetings. On one of our walks along the Norfolk coast we decided to publish the book ourselves to ensure that we could easily keep it available to readers.

It has been a special delight to find a creative team to share in our enterprise – in meetings around restaurant tables as well as in studios, by webcam and email: Marianne Hartley for her creative and wholehearted work in designing the book, Steven Appleby for his distinctive drawn world, John Dawson for editing from Nairobi with an international perspective, and our flexible and patient printers, Biddles of King's Lynn. We met Marianne during world peace teachings given by the Dalai Lama in Graz, Austria; she met Steven with his sons on a train to Glasgow; John was recommended by a long-time colleague who had only worked with him via email. This team has transformed the project with enthusiasm, humour and commitment.

We would particularly like to welcome and thank Martin Farrell of get2thepoint, who has brought fresh energy to the final stages in drafting the book, adding tips and stories, and acting as co-publisher. He will join us in our offer of help to individuals and organizations in bringing the principles of *Meeting Together* into reality in their work.

Lois Graessle and George Gawlinski

HOW TO GET HELP
TO IMPROVE YOUR MEETINGS

In addition to using the book, you can find more tips, guidelines and other helpful tools on our website, to which new ideas and information are being added all the time. Take a look at **www.meetingtogether.org.**

We are also happy to discuss with you the variety of ways in which we could help you as an individual or in a group or organization, through coaching, training, organizational review, and facilitation.

Contact us at:
Martin Farrell
get2thepoint
+44 (0)20 8404 8661
martin.farrell@get2thepoint.org
or
Lois Graessle
Planning Together Associates
+44 (0)20 8995 0244
lois@planningtogether.com

HOW TO ORDER
MEETING TOGETHER
AND PLANNING TOGETHER

Planning Together Press
281A Wootton Road
King's Lynn
Norfolk PE30 3AR
United Kingdom
+44 (0)1553 671 620

sales@planningtogether.com
or through any bookseller, or online through Amazon.com and others.
Special rates are available for bulk orders and for buying both books.

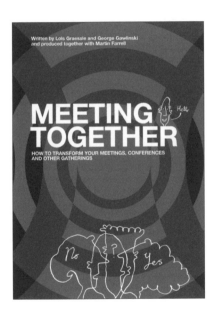
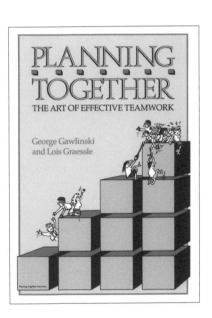

Meeting Together and *Planning Together* are companion volumes to help you improve your working together.

Planning Together: The art of effective teamwork, the authors' first book, has become a classic in the not-for-profit sector for generations of managers. *Planning Together* presents a model of cooperative planning that may be used by any group of people working together as a team – whether at senior management level in a national organization or in a non-hierarchical voluntary project. It is particularly directed to those working in the service sector, both public and private.